AGELESS INDIA - 2

artnfact

AGELESS INDIA - 2

SPIRIT OF INDIA

Curated by
National Museum, New Delhi

Series Editor
MALVIKA SINGH

LIMITED
EDITIONS

AN IMPRINT OF
ACADEMIC FOUNDATION

INTRODUCTION TO THE SERIES

This series of Notebooks was conceived as a vibrant and energetic representation of India, manifesting images of her past and present, her remarkable and infinite civilisation with its endless layers of diversity merging and melding into one another, creating a fabric of seamless transitions laced with overlaps of buoyant contradictions that are often unpredictable and mysterious, allowing for flights of the imagination, and leaving 'room for wonder'.

Through the pages of *Ageless India*, this extraordinary and finely nuanced, ever-evolving and contemporary destination on earth, continues to draw into its complex unstitched folds, the many stories and experiences, the influences and ideas that emerge from a 'planet', continually revolving ecliptically on its firm axis, sharing experience and endorsing a sublime unity in exciting and invigorating diversity.

The voyeur in us can use these books to exchange notes, share ideas, articulate intangible reflections in words, and more, to leave them as 'memories' that can be savoured today, as well as in the years to come, by family and friends, to keep the connect of the past with the future alive.

Ageless India will showcase the personalised 'India' of men and women impassioned by her many 'plots' and 'sub-plots', using the skill of their hands and eyes to capture for posterity, her changing avatars, her multiple expressions. The series will be infinite...

Malvika Singh
New Delhi 2015

AGELESS INDIA - 2

SPIRIT OF INDIA

National Museum, New Delhi, houses an impressive collection of over 210,000 artifacts representing 5,000 years of Indian art and craftsmanship. The collection includes sculpture in stone, bronze, terracotta and wood, a large collection of miniature paintings and manuscripts, coins, arms and armour, jewellery, textile, costumes and anthropological objects. The notebook features 53 objects from the National Museum and presents some basic information about each. Every page meets you with an extraordinary object from the past.

Series Editor
MALVIKA SINGH

PREHISTORY

The Harappan civilisation which thrived along the mighty Indus river, also known as Indus Valley civilisation, is believed to be one of the Old World civilisations, much like Egypt and Mesopotamia.

Known as the Bronze Age, several objects made of copper based alloys have been found in Harappan sites. The famous 'dancing girl', a bronze figurine, reveals the hairstyle and ornaments of the period. One of the most remarkable seals that was unearthed, depicts a man in a yogic posture surrounded by animals, compelling the speculation that this could be 'Pasupati', an early form of Rudra or Siva. The wealth and variety of objects discovered offer a comprehensive lesson of that past and its influence on the culture of India.

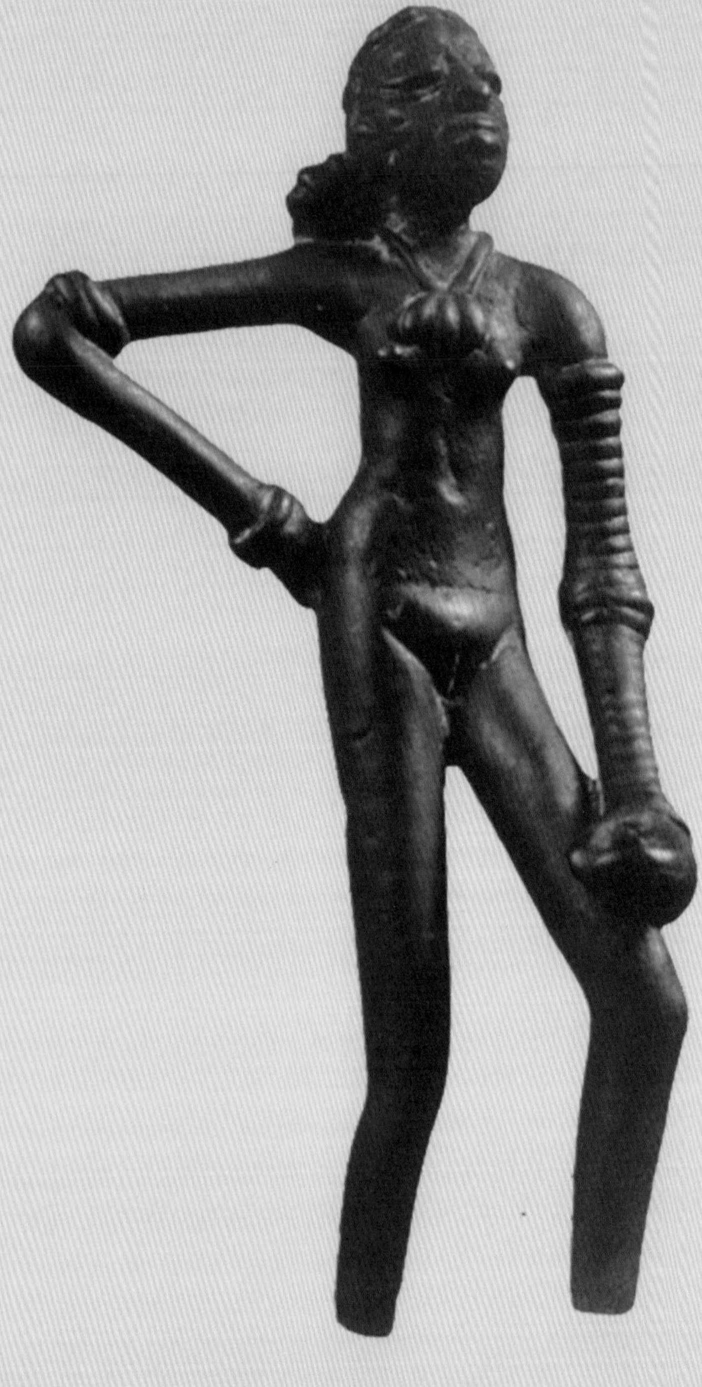

Dancing Girl
2700-2100 BCE
Bronze
Acc no – Hr. 5721/195

From this masterpiece, we know that the Harappans were skilled in metallurgy and knew how to cast alloys of metals using the lost wax process. The tilted head and flexed knees, bent right arm dramatically resting on her hip and the other hand holding a bowl suggest a dancing pose.

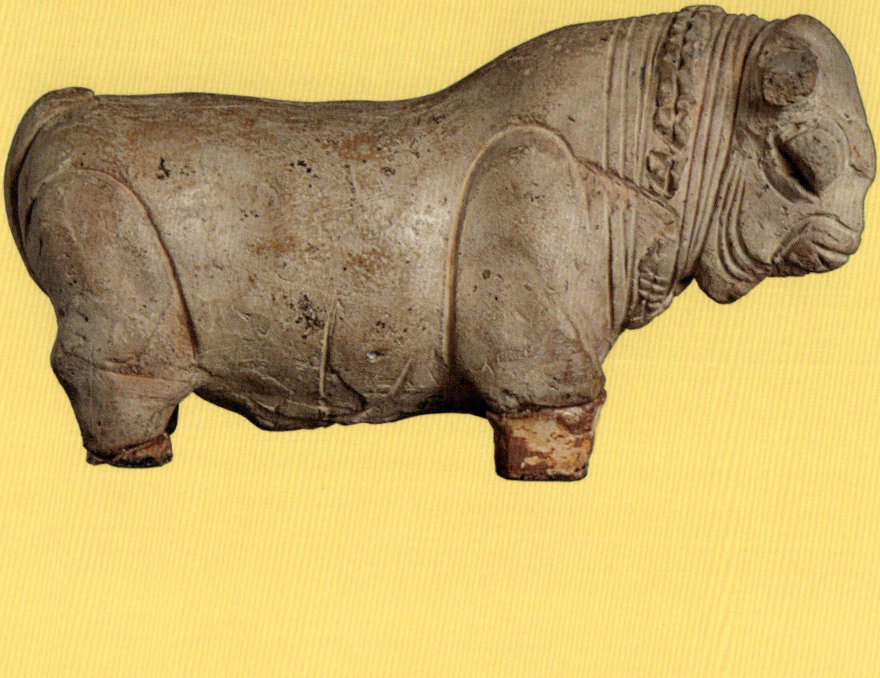

Un-Humped Bull
2700 BCE
Terracotta
Acc no – V.S 1539/234

Depictions of the bull on seals or figurines have always been done very artistically. This terracotta bull figurine is entirely handmade. Probably a knife was used to shape parts of the body and its minute details, after which a thin cream slip was put over the entire figurine.

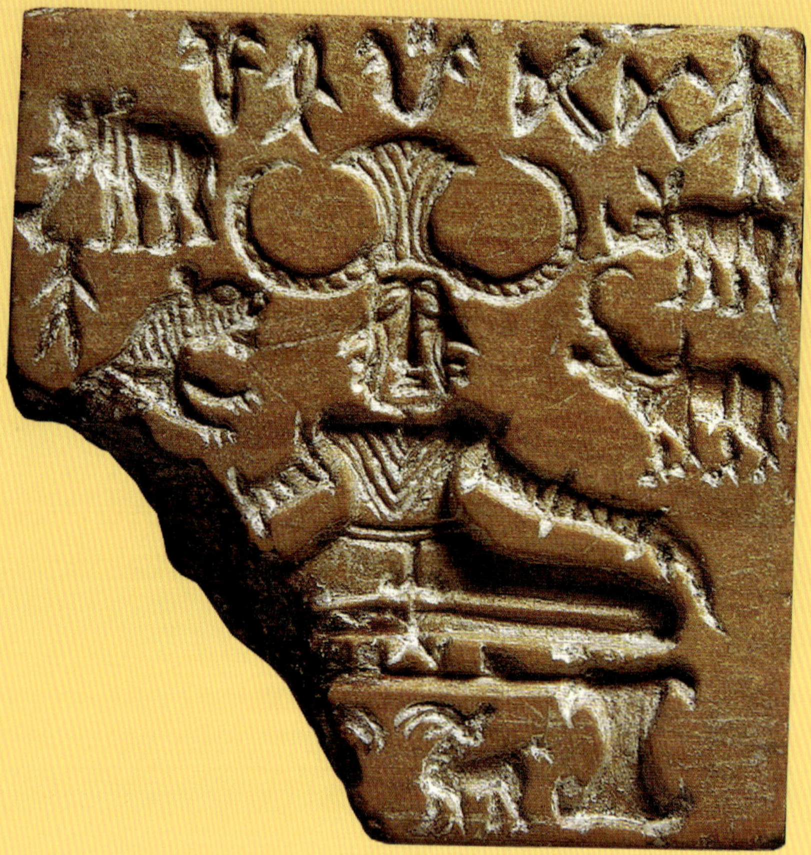

Pasupati or Proto-Siva
2700–2100 BCE
Terracotta
Acc. No - DK 5175/143

One of the most important industries of Harappa was seal cutting and there are several masterpieces of this art-form that remain. This seal represents a seated man wearing a prominent head gear with buffalo horns. Some scholars have identified the figure as the earliest representation of Siva; in his form as Pasupati.

ARCHAEOLOGY

Archaeology opens up the secrets of a world past, through discovery and scrutiny of the material found through excavation. The environmental conditions and rituals prevalent in a particular period, the various kinds of gems, tools, pottery and sculpture that are unearthed tell a story of human life in another age. Myths and legends are manifested in the elaborate sculptures, as are representations of Gods and Goddesses.

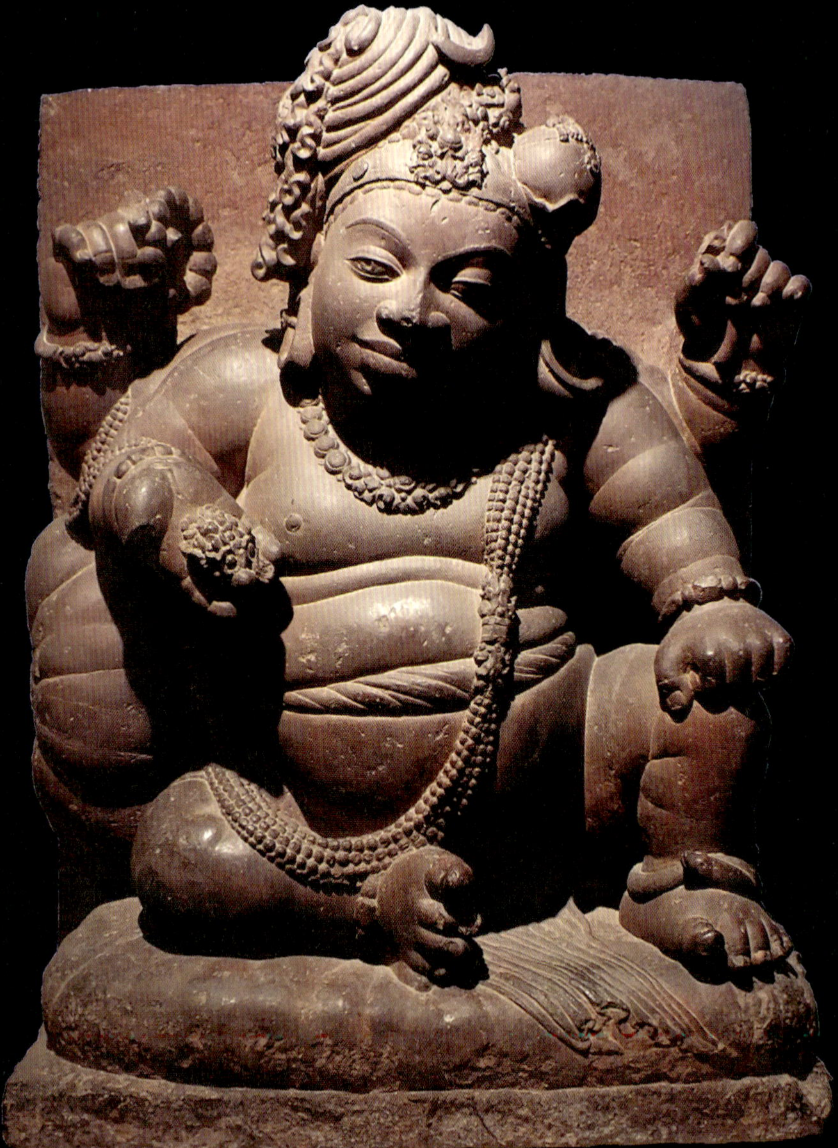

Siva Vamana
5th century CE
Red Sandstone
Acc No – L. 77/2

Siva is rarely seen in this unique form. He is shown as a seated Vamana (dwarf) here on a cushion against a large, round decorated pillow. He is wearing a Sarpa Nupura (snake-like anklet) and a massive strand of twisted pearls. A large circular earring, usually seen on his consort, Parvati, rests on his shoulder.

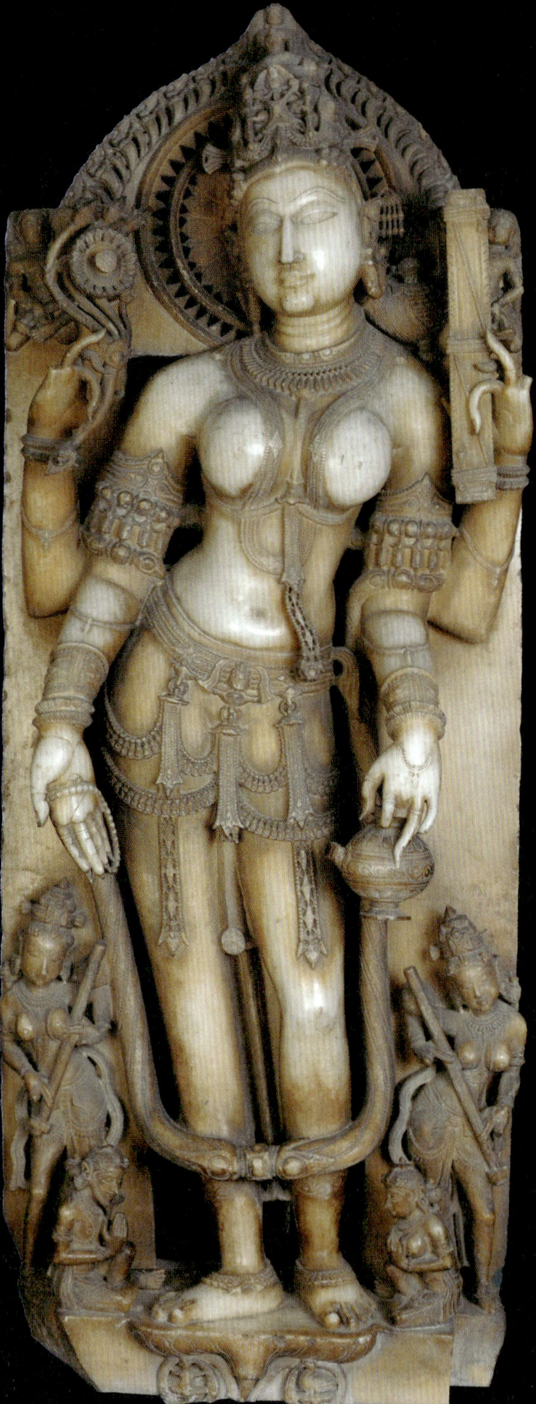

ARCHAEOLOGY

Saraswati
12th century CE
Marble
Acc no – 1-6/278

Saraswati is the goddess of learning, music, eloquence and intelligence in the Brahmanical Hindu pantheon. She is also considered Shakti (female power) of the great creator, Brahma. This sculpture is a highly sophisticated and a delicate work of sculptural art made in white marble, representing Saraswati in the form of Vagdevi of the Jain pantheon.

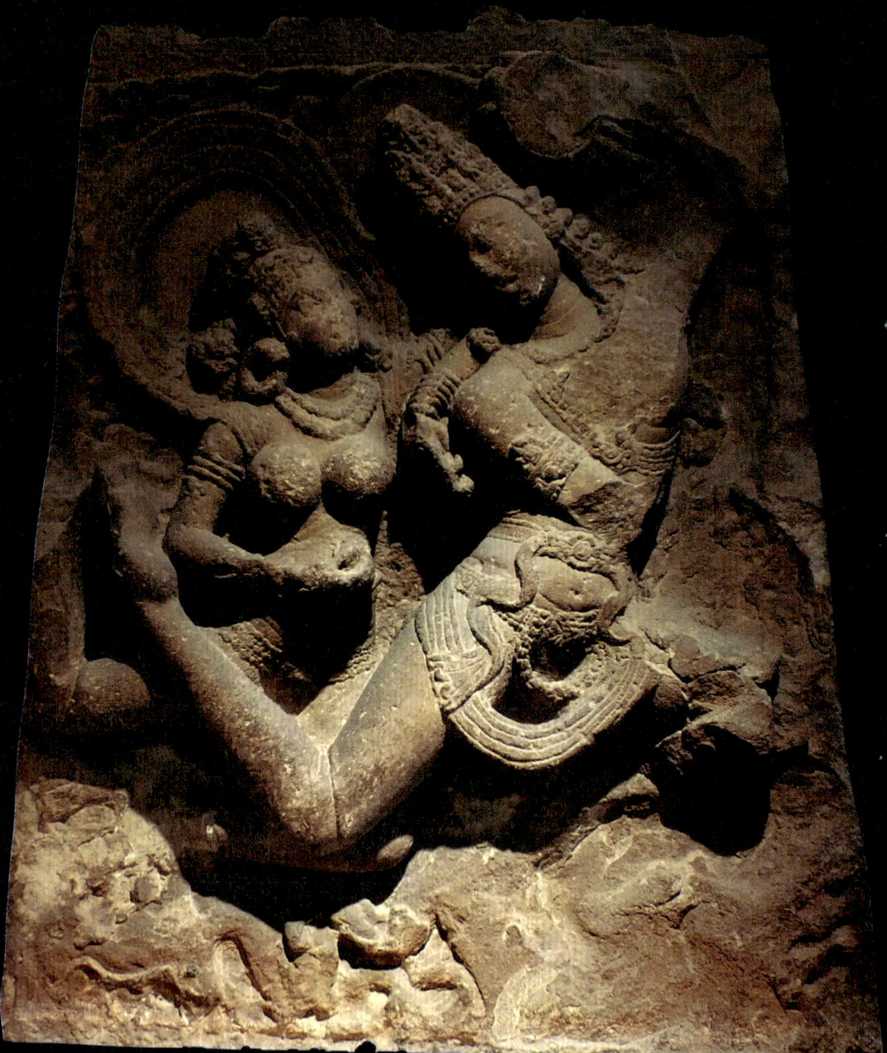

ARCHAEOLOGY

Flying Celestials
7th century CE
Sandstone
Acc no – L. 55.22

This panel is one from the rare Chalukyan temple ceiling. This ceiling slab depicts a flying celestial couple. The soft fluttering garments and depiction of clouds suggest a skyward movement of the divine couple.

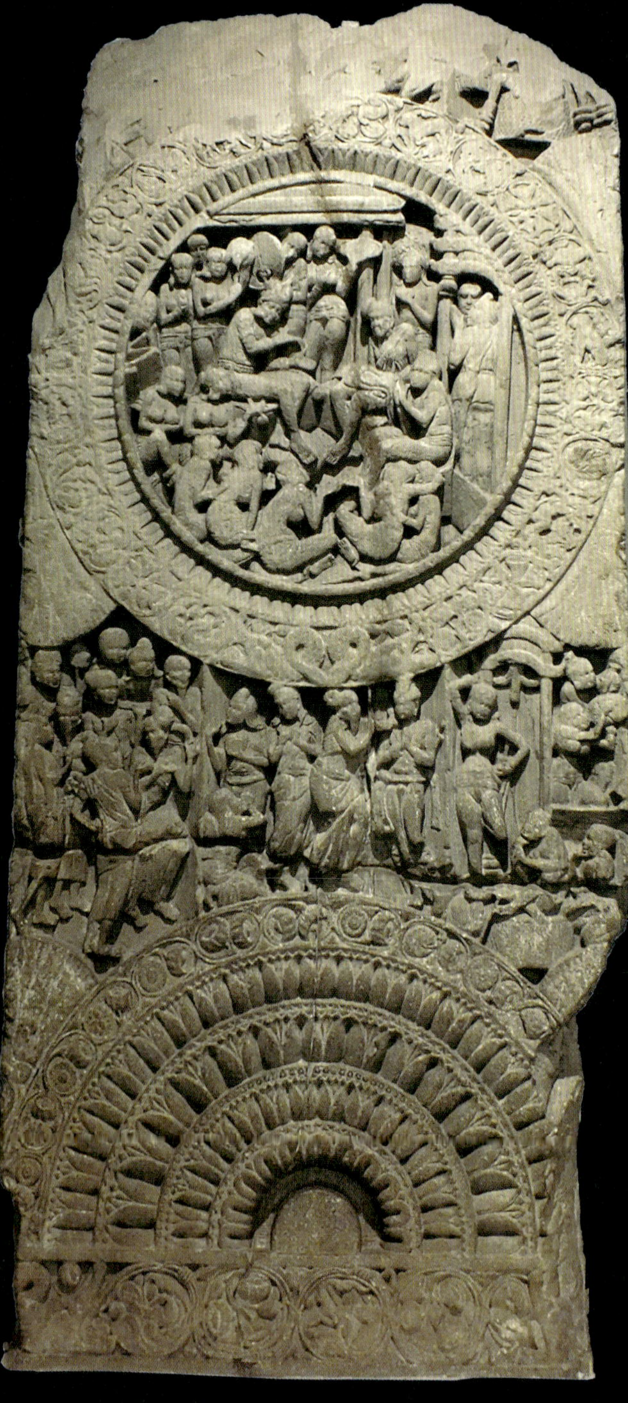

ARCHAEOLOGY

Railing Pillar Depicting Asita's Visit
1st-2nd century CE
Stone
Acc no – 70.L/4

Sage Asita visited King Suddhodhana at his palace when Buddha was born as Prince Siddhartha in the Shakya clan. Upon seeing the auspicious signs on the baby's body, Asita prophesied that he would either become a great king or a great monk. The latter came true. The episode is shown on this relief panel made of limestone.

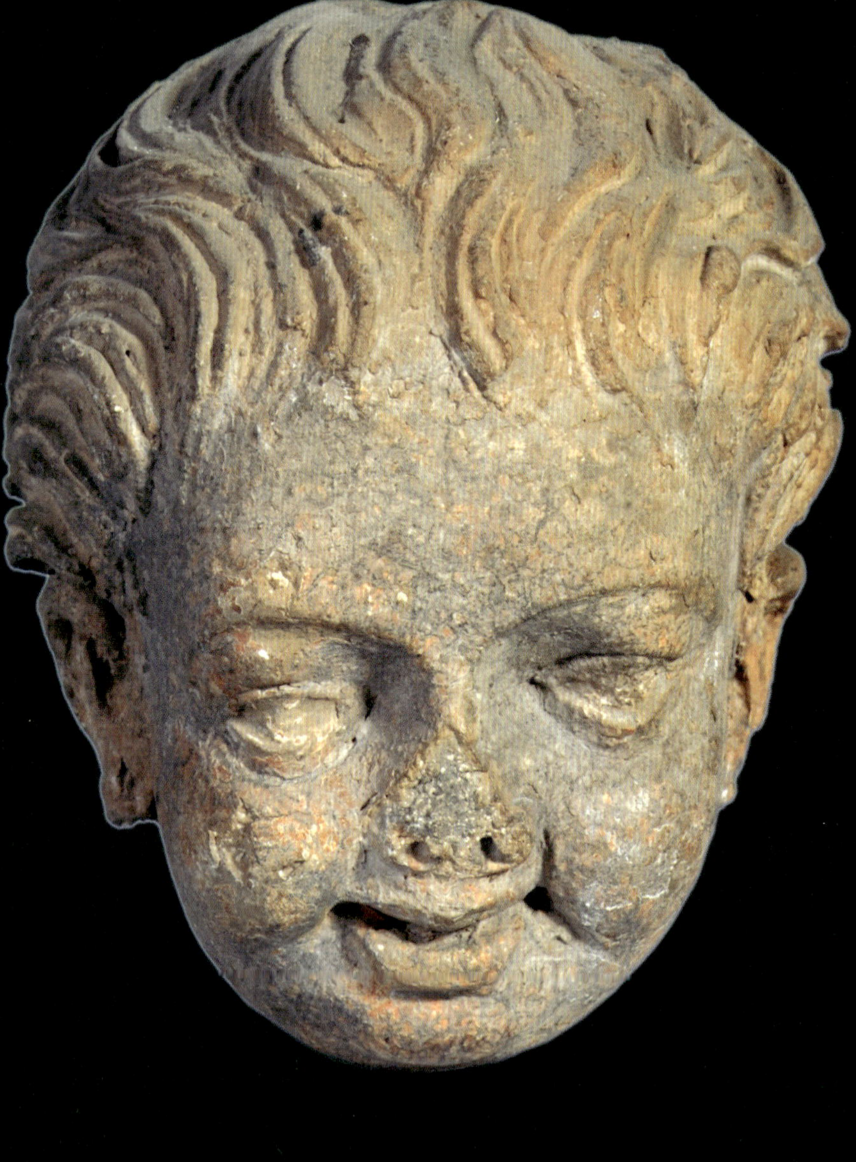

ARCHAEOLOGY

Laughing Boy Head
3rd-4th century CE
Stucco
Acc no – 876jn. 16 F.28

The Greco–Roman art that developed in the region of Gandhara in the 1st century, evolved into what was termed 'Late Gandhara', or 'Afghan Art' in the 3rd to the early 5th century CE. This small portrait head of a boy with full cheeks, wide open eyes and a slightly open mouth, renders a very pleasing countenance. The wavy hair is combed back, similar to other Gandharan examples.

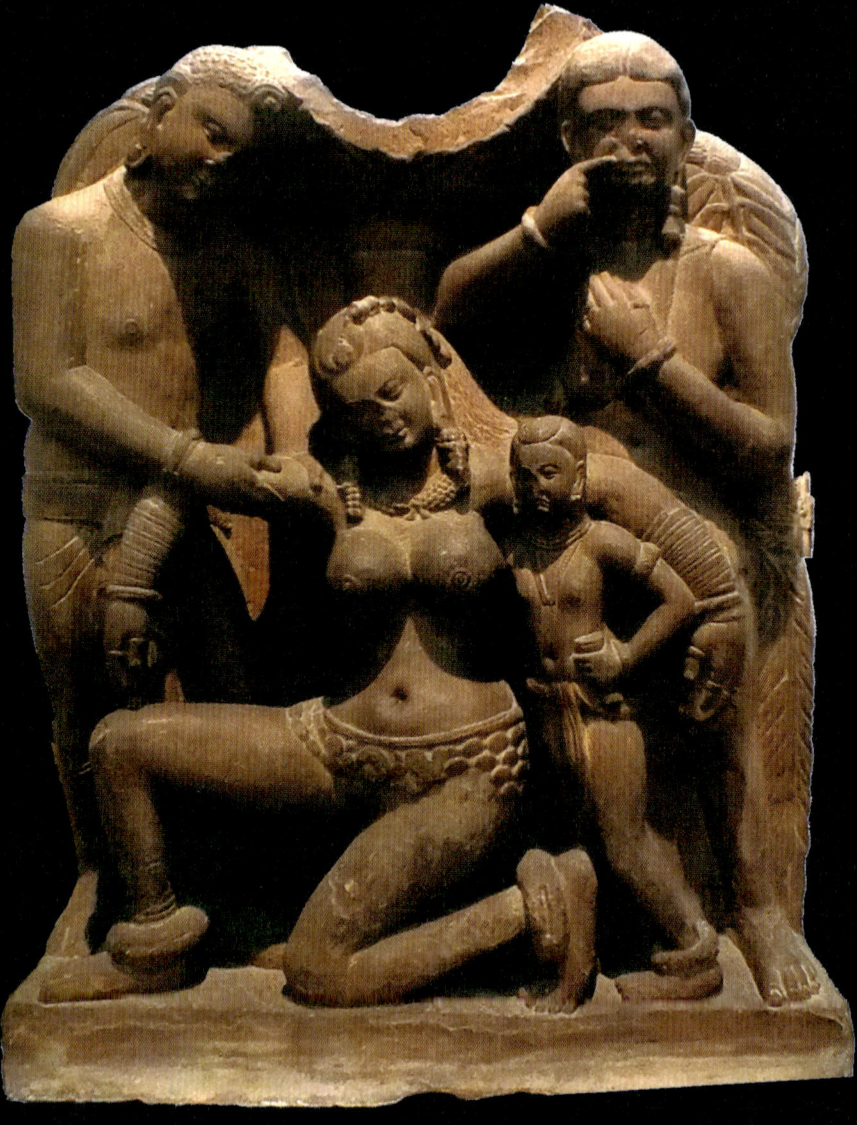

Vasantsena
2nd century CE
Red Sandstone
Acc no – 2800

Vasantsena is the heroine of the Sanskrit drama, *Mricchakatikam*, believed to be written by Shudraka between 2nd century BCE and 5th century CE. This sculpture shows the first scene from the play where the heroine is being followed in the dark by Shakara and his retinue. Vasantsena is an opulent courtesan, the fairest gem of Ujjain, and this is indicated by the attendant figure holding a *chattra*/parasol over her, which can be seen on the reverse of this relief panel.

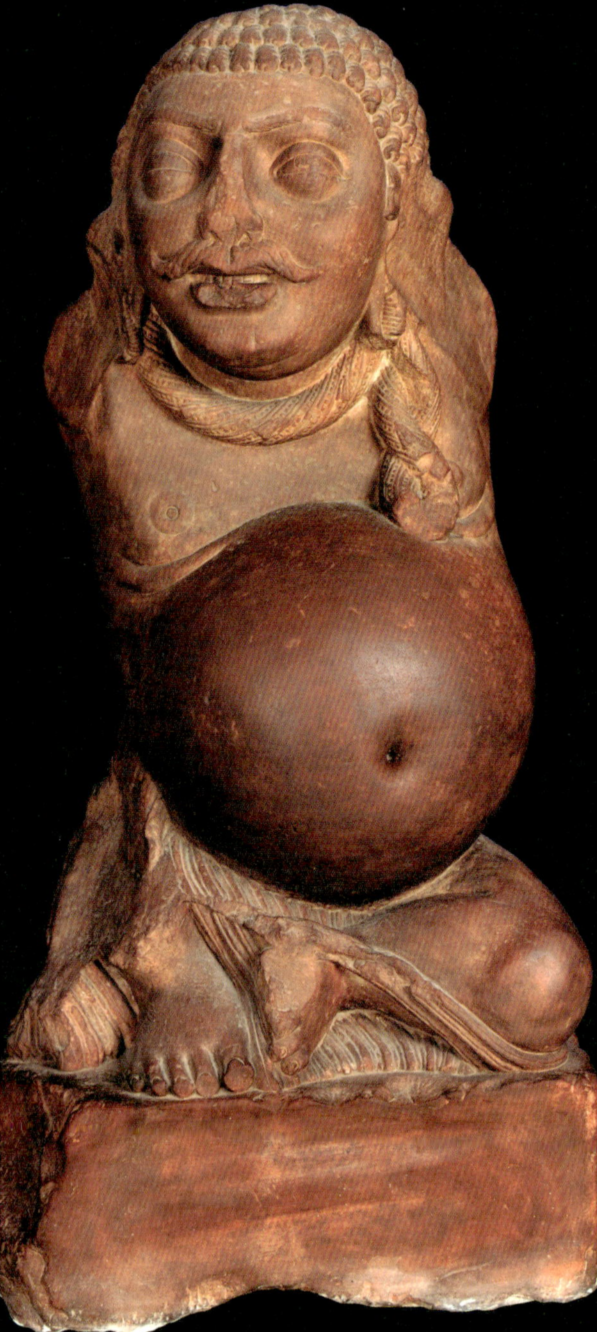

ARCHAEOLOGY

Kubera
2nd century CE
Red Sandstone
Acc no – 59.530/2

In Hindu mythology, Kubera is the God of wealth and prosperity and is the guardian of the North. His bare body is dominated by a voluminous stomach that rests against his left thigh. This sculpture was discovered at Ahichchhatra (in present-day Uttar Pradesh), a site identified with the capital of ancient Panchala of Mahabharata fame. However, stylistically, historians assert that it was made at Mathura.

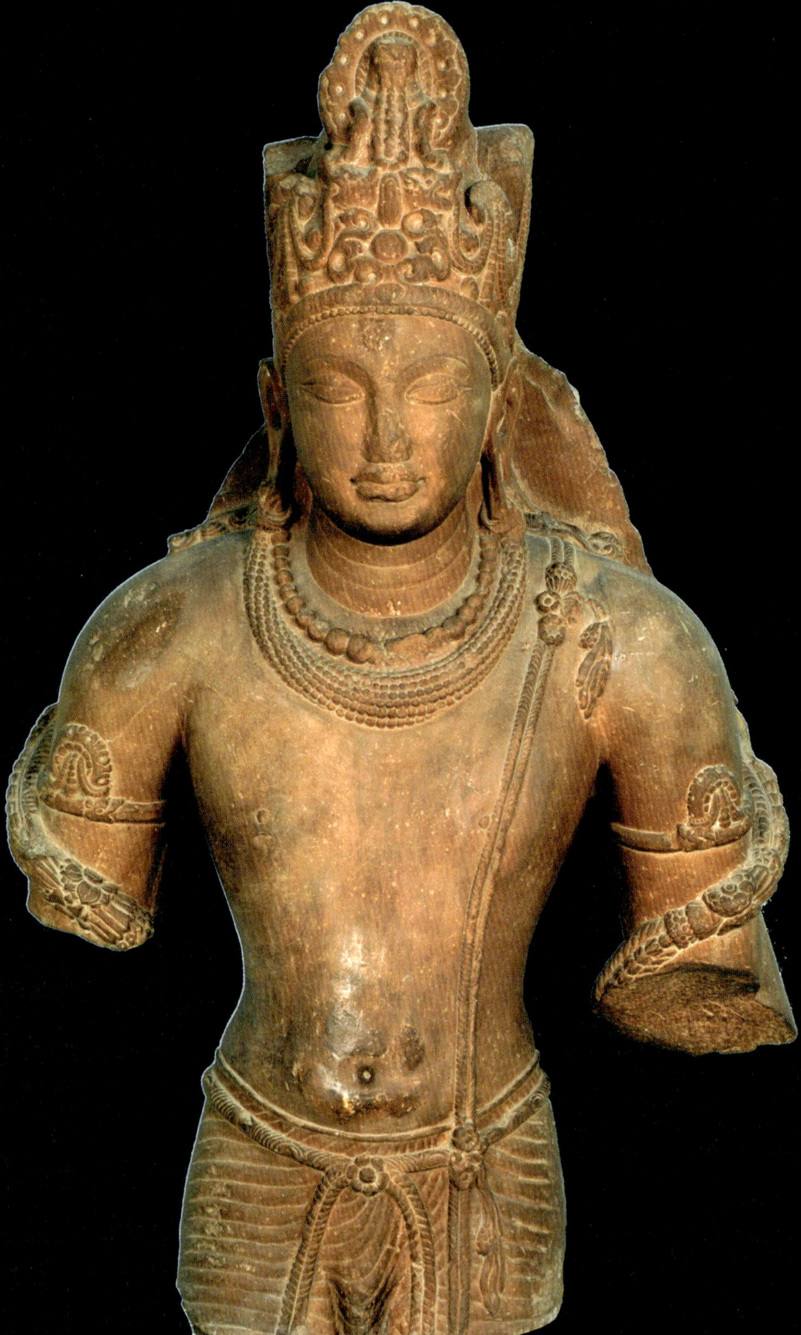

ARCHAEOLOGY

Vishnu
Mid-5th century CE
Red Sandstone
Acc no – E.6

This impressive Vishnu depicts the diety as four-armed, wearing a jewelled crown (*kritikamukuta*), the sacred thread (*yajnopavita*) (with fastenings at the left shoulder and the waist) and a long garland made of flowers (*vanamala*). When complete, this image must have had a large halo (*prabhavali*). The depiction of arched eyebrows, gently lowered eyes, full lips, half-closed eyes, rounded chin and the three conventional folds around the neck are all characteristics of the 5th century CE monumental images of Vishnu of the Gupta period that display great aesthetic excellence.

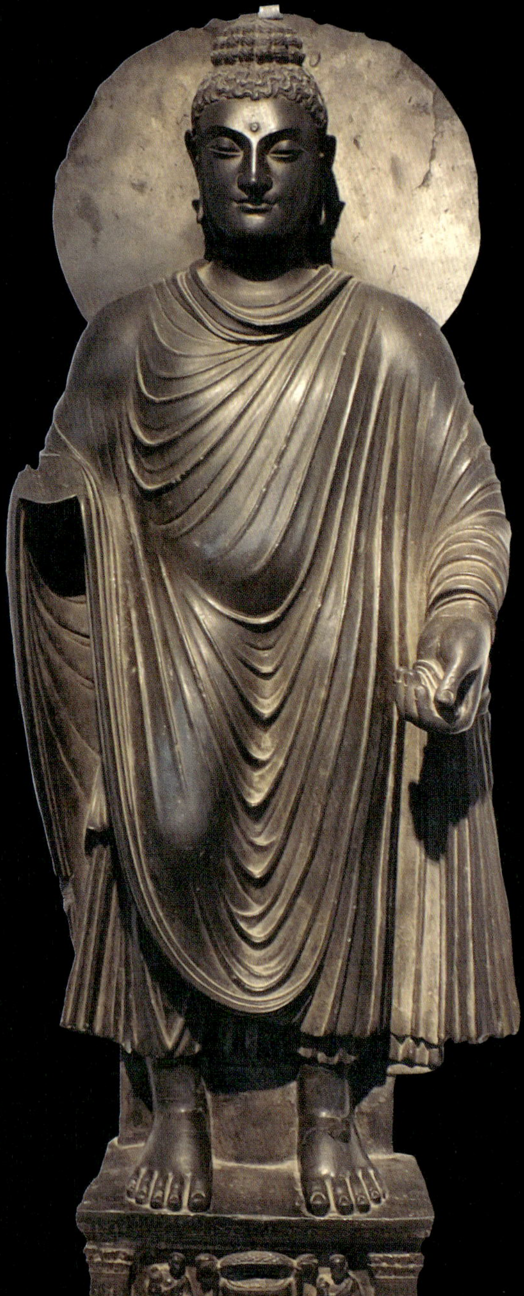

ARCHAEOLOGY

Standing Buddha
2nd century CE
Schist Stone
Acc no – 87.1153

This sculpture is typically Gandharan in style, marked by the long flowing drapery placed loosely on the body with heavy schematic folds. The right hand, which is mostly lost, was in *Abhaya Mudra* (the 'Fear not' pose), a typical feature of the standing Buddhas. He is holding the hem of the *Sanghati* (garment) in his left hand. With the *Abhaya Mudra*, he assures his devotees of ultimate salvation.

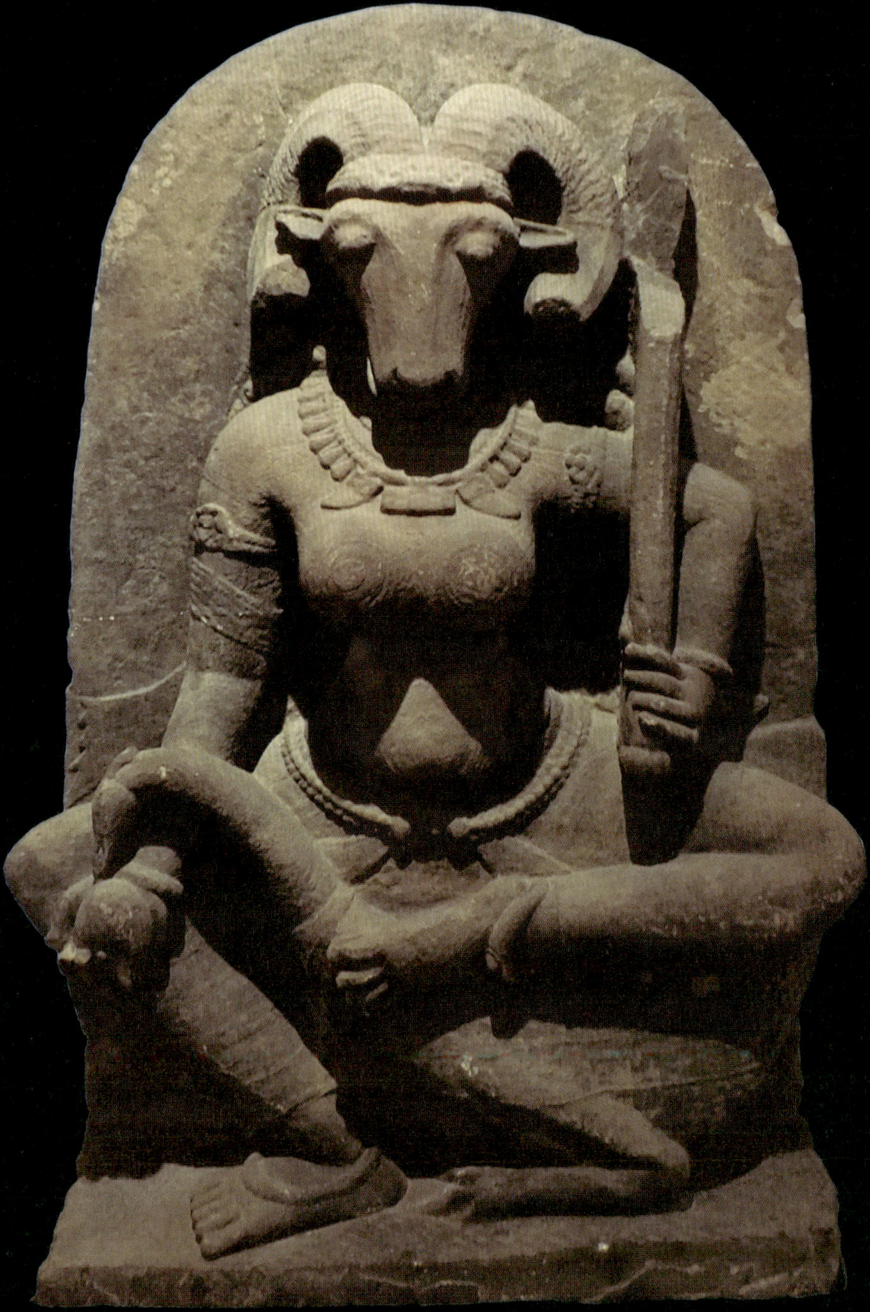

ARCHAEOLOGY

Yogini
10th century CE
Stone
Acc no – M.13/20

This Yogini sculpture belongs to a site named Lokhari, a village in the Banda district in the Bundelkhand region of Uttar Pradesh. Esoteric form of worship was prevalent in that region since 10th century CE. Yogini Vrishanana (buffalo-headed goddess) sits against an un-ornamented stele in Lalitasana with a club in her left hand and a *Bilva* fruit in her right hand. Her vehicle is a swan that pecks on the fruit in her right hand.

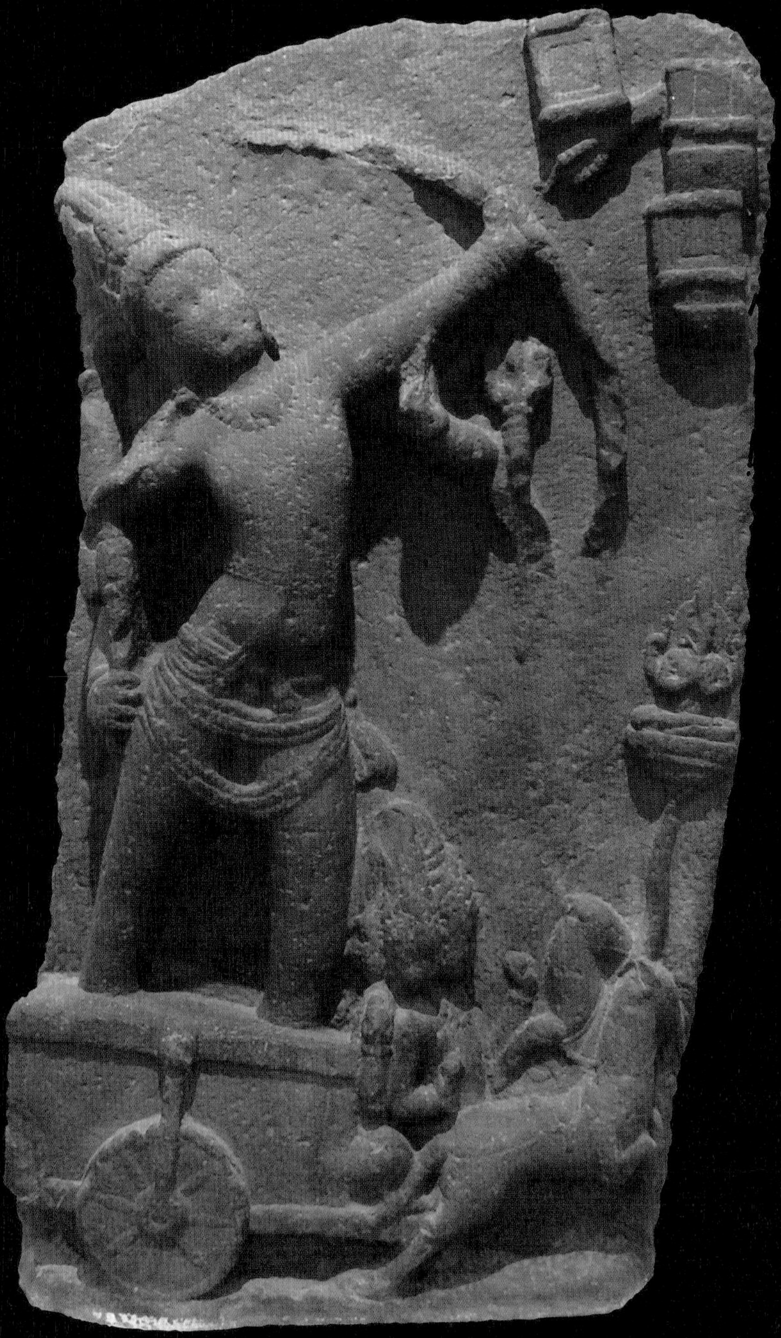

ARCHAEOLOGY

Tripurantaka
8th century CE
Stone
Acc no – L.55.17

Siva as Tripurantaka is accredited with destroying three mythical cities of the Asura (Demons). This panel depicts one of the eight legends narrating Siva's role as the destroyer of evil, the Tripura-samhara (destruction of the three citadels). It is said in the legend that the demon, Taraka had three offsprings named Taarakaakshа, Kamalaaksha and Vidyunmaali.

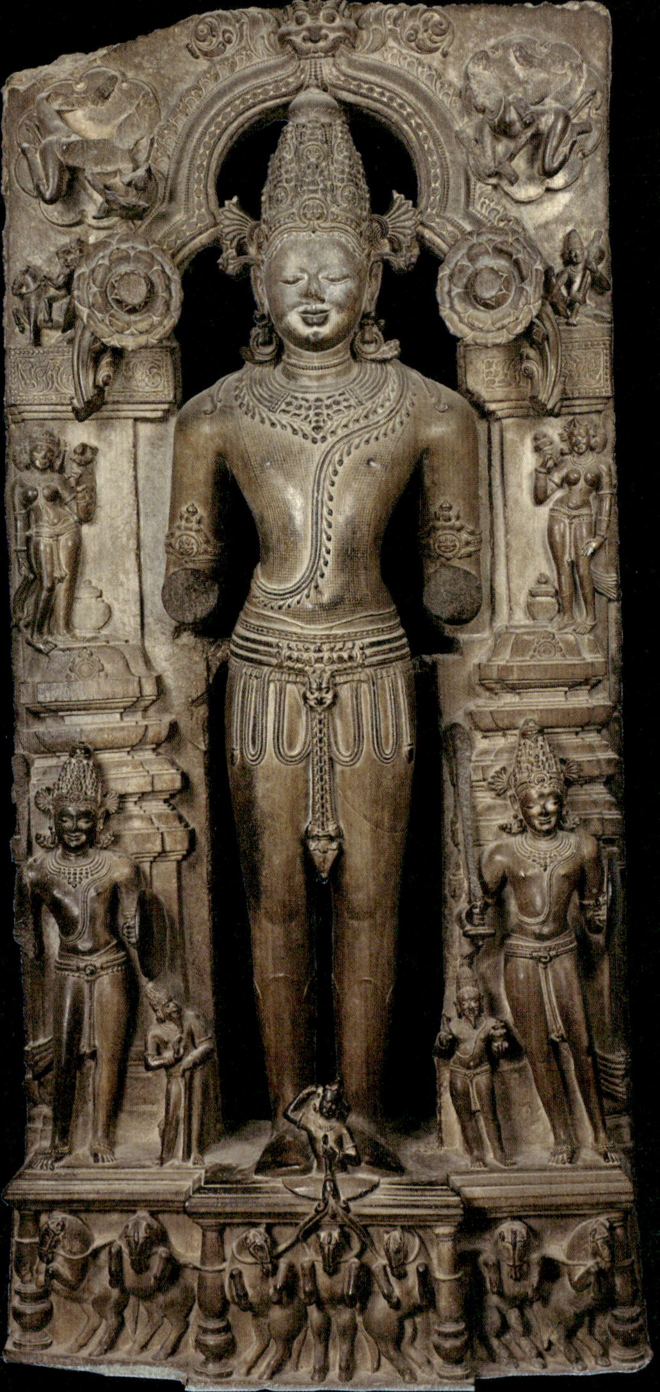

ARCHAEOLOGY

Surya
13th century CE
Khondolite stone
Acc no - 50.178

This is one of the finest sculptures from the Sun temple of Konarak and may have once been installed for worship in the sanctum. Surya is depicted standing, holding full blown lotuses in both hands, riding on a chariot driven by charioteer Aruna, drawn by seven galloping horses. Surya is the source of light, warmth, life and knowledge, and is the solar deity from the early period of the Rigveda.

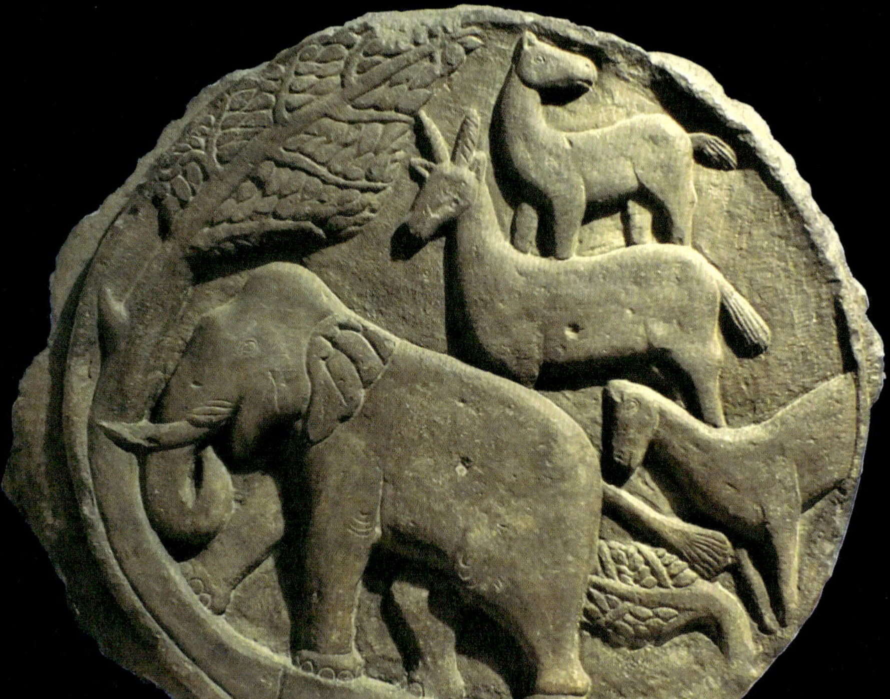

ARCHAEOLOGY

Fragment of a Railing Pillar (Medallion)
2nd century BCE
Sandstone
Acc no – 80.751

It is the central medallion of a railing post, carved on both the sides. It represents a Jataka story depicting a moving elephant, probably uprooting a tree, and three deers at his back in fearful mood on the side, and a Yaksha figure on the other side.

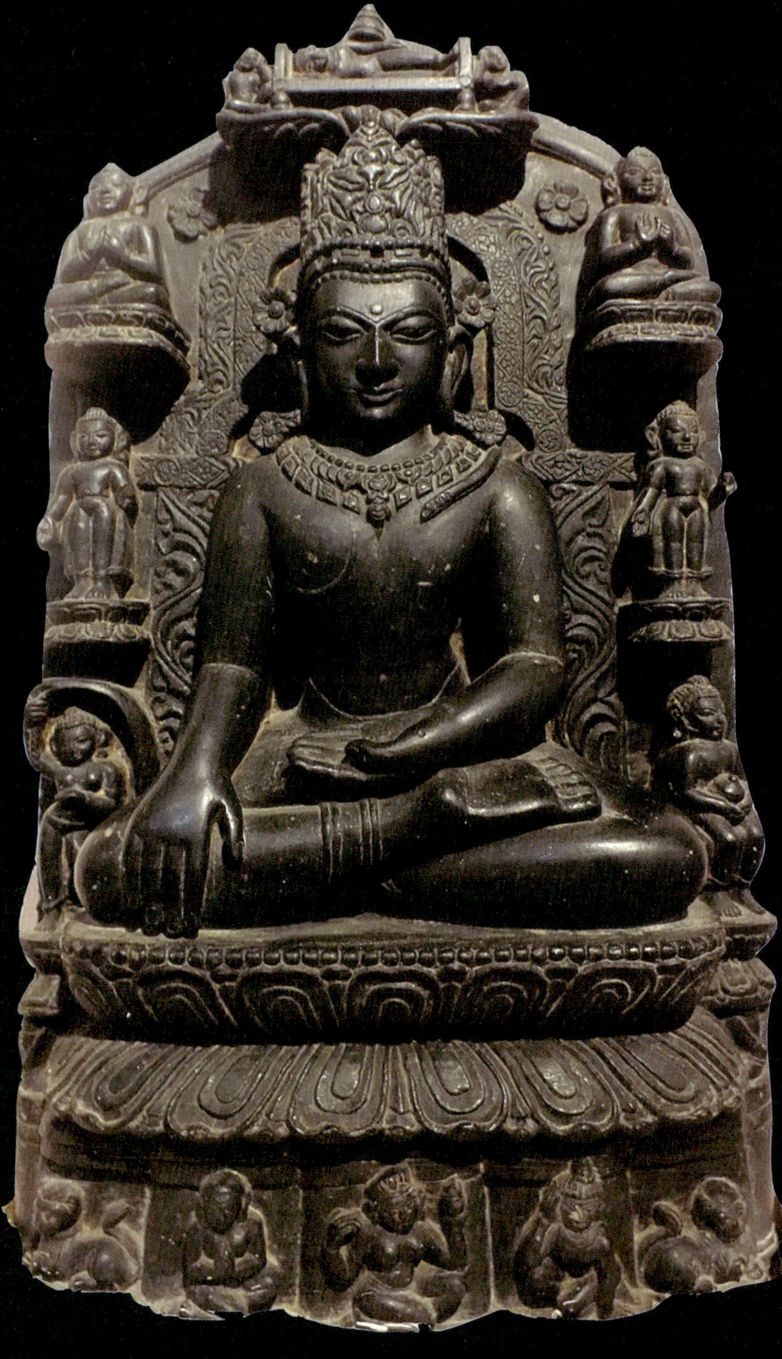

Crowned Buddha
12th century CE
Stone
Acc no – 63.645

The Pala emperors were Buddhists, their seals bore the wheel and deer emblem associated with the first sermon by Buddha at Sarnath. The Buddhist icons, 8th century onwards, only present the crowned form with elaborate ornaments, which is a marked digression from the original Buddhist theory of abstinence from material possessions.

BRONZE

The fine art of bronze casting proves the technical excellence of artisans in metallurgy in ancient India. Since the Harappan civilisation, the lost-wax process (Madhucchista Vidhana) has been used to cast bronze. Several artefacts from the Shunga, Kushana and Ikshvaku periods have been discovered, but it was the Gupta period that triumphed in the casting of metal images on a large scale, spreading the skill to other regions.

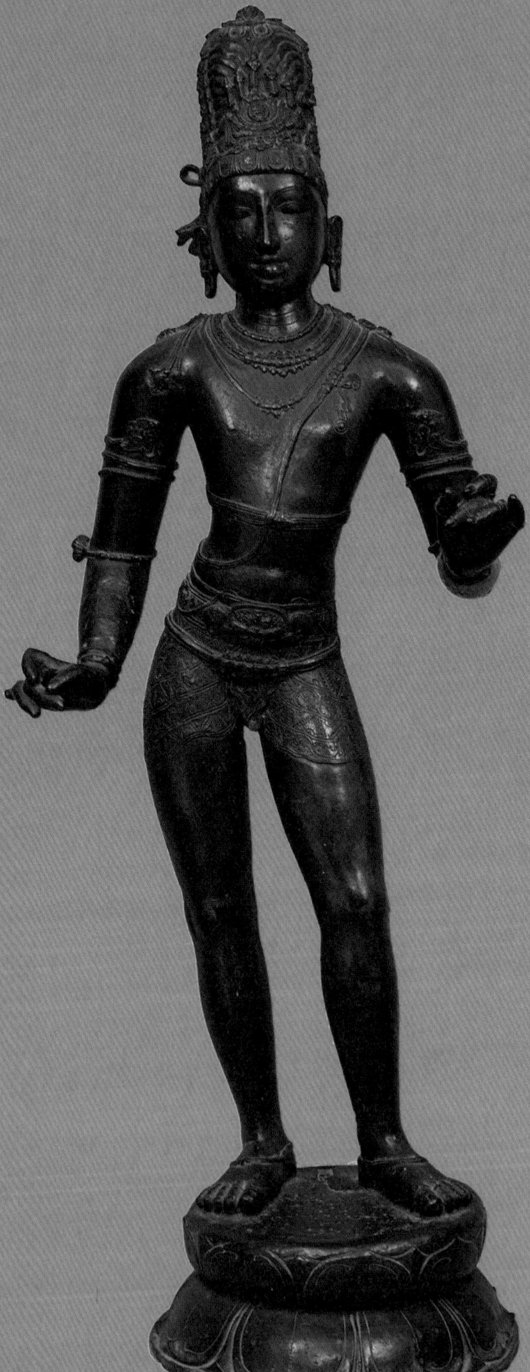

BRONZE

Siva-Tripurantaka
9th century CE
Bronze
Acc no – 82.223

Siva in Tripurantaka form is presented in a warrior pose, riding a chariot, of which the four Vedas are the horses, and Brahma the charioteer. Siva is shown ready to shoot an arrow to destroy the impregnable three cities of the demons, releasing them from the bondage of ignorance into immortality.

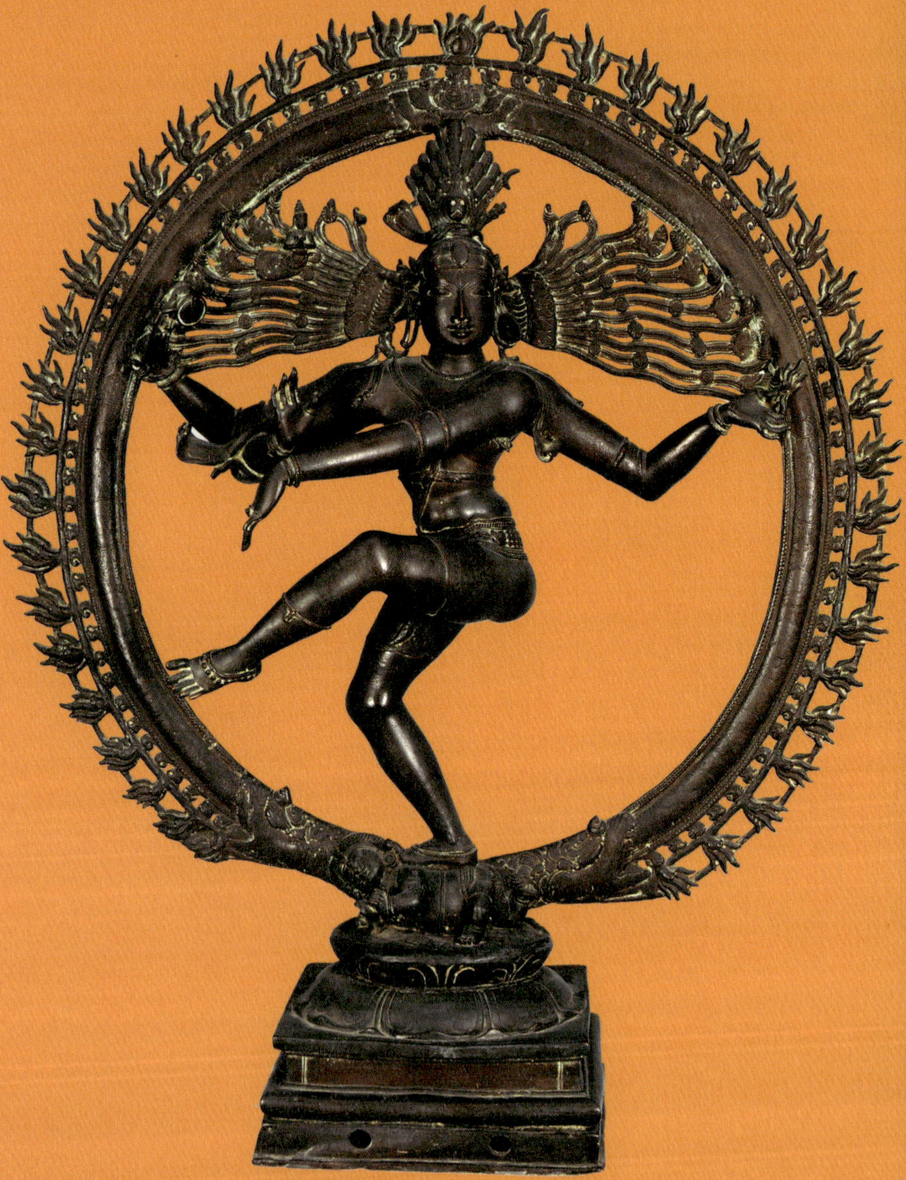

RONZE

ataraja
2th century CE
ronze
cc no – 56.2/1

ataraja, the Lord of Dance, represents the essential aspects of Siva: reation, preservation, destruction nd grace. The dance he performs s that of bliss or *ananda tandava*.

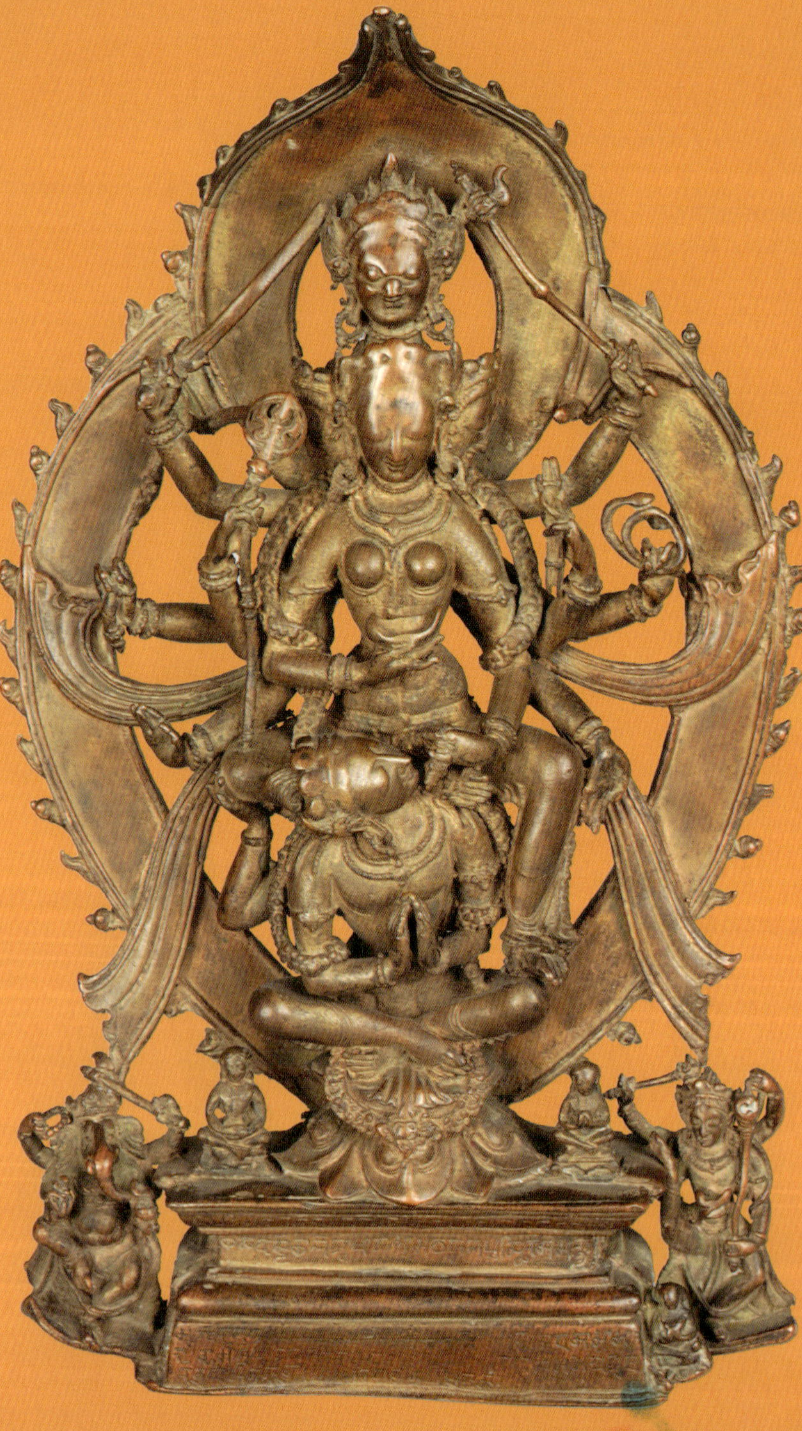

BRONZE

Svachchhanda Bhairavi
10th century CE
Bronze
Acc no – 64.102

This is a very fine example of the early medieval art of the Himalayan region. Some scholars identify this bronze as Svachchhanda Bhairavi, while others consider it as the female counterpart of Sadashiva and some suggest it is a representation of Mahabhairavi. The undesiphered inscription on the pedestal in Sarada characters places it in 1,000 CE.

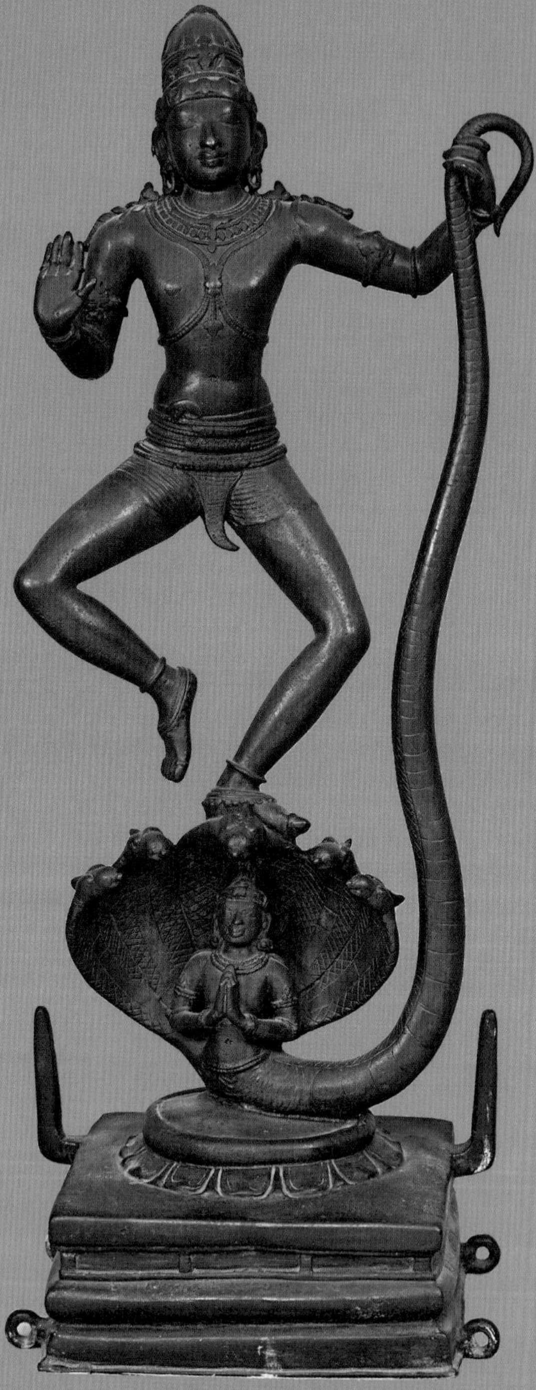

BRONZE

Kaliya-Mardan Krishna
10th century CE
Bronze
Acc no – 70.11

This is an elegant bronze image of Krishna dancing on the serpent hood of Kaliya naga. It represents the story of how Krishna learnt that the village cattle were being poisoned when they drank from waters of the Kalindi River. Being the protector of the cowherd community, the young Krishna finds that the culprit is the proud Kaliya naga or serpent demon.

PAINTINGS

In ancient India, painting, architecture and sculpture was influenced by prehistoric rock paintings. Some of the Stone Age rock paintings, like the Bhimbetka rock shelters are approximately 30,000 years old. The later Mughal painting styles are a blend of Persian miniature techniques and older Indian traditions. From the 17th century onwards, this basic style changed from atelier to royal atelier with local additions of motif and pattern.

The Mughal school is showcased in a dated folio of the *Babar Nama*, autobiography of Emperor Babur (1598). It is a remarkable portfolio. In other works, Shahjahan is shown in a profusely illustrated painting that picturises the marriage of his son, Dara Shikoh. The kingdoms of Rajasthan too, had a miniature painting tradition in different styles. Rajput art focused primarily on religious themes and on the epics. Portraiture was mastered by the ateliers.

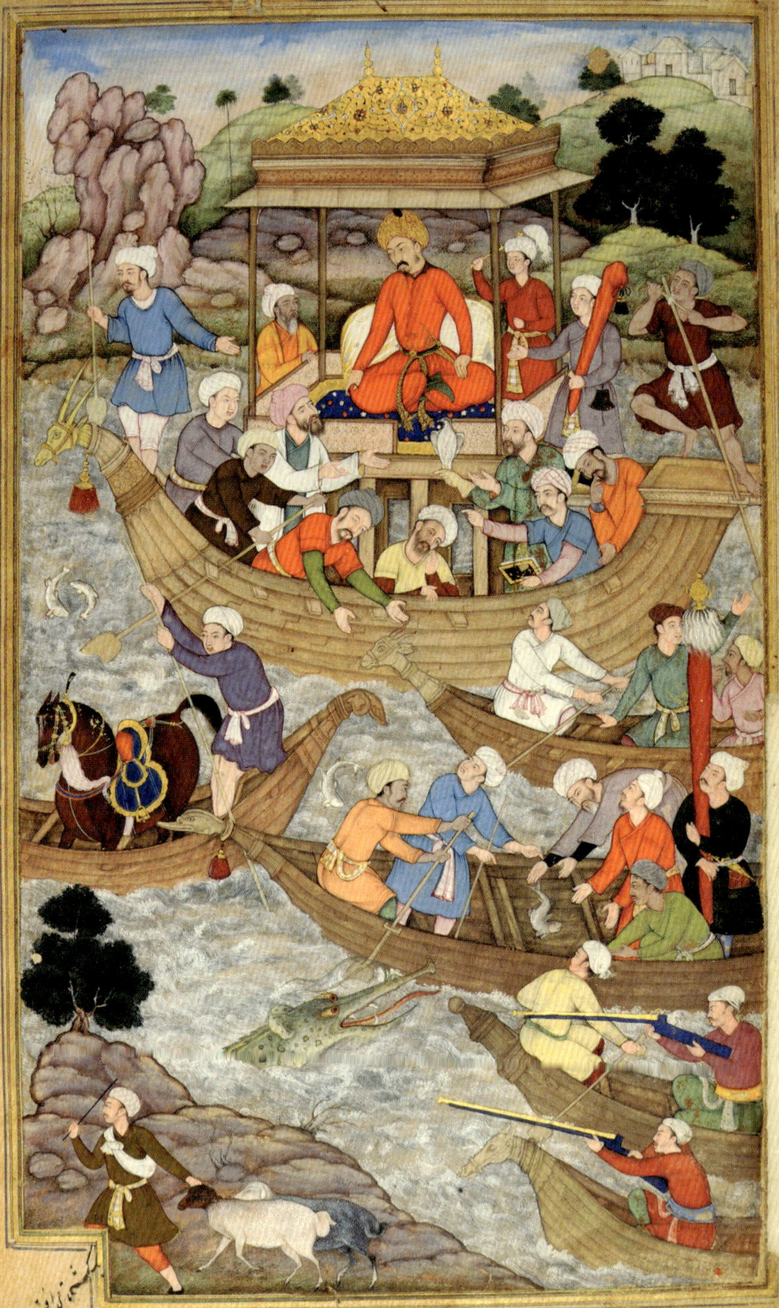

Folio of Babur Nama
c. 1598 CE
Paper
Acc no – 50.336

This painting depicts a scene of April 14, 1529, when Babur crossed the River Saun using a bridge of boats. Babur is sitting on the platform of Gunjaish surrounded by attendants. In the middle of the paintings is a boat onto which has leapt a fish. Two soldiers armed with muskets are firing at the crocodile. All the onlookers are sharing the excitement, which the incident has provided. Babur is sitting beneath a pavilion constructed on the larger boat. He is the highest figure in the painting, establishing his status as master of all the surveys.

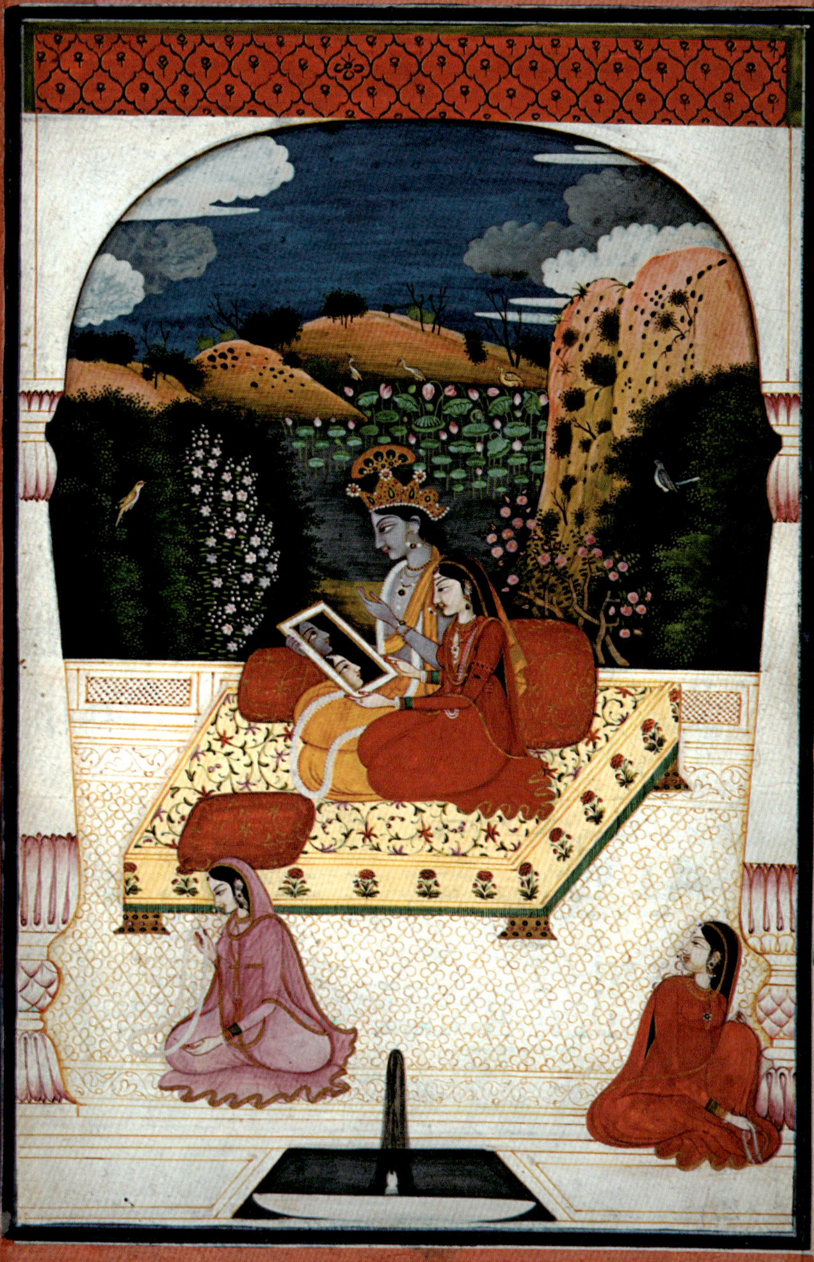

Krishna looking into a Mirror
Late 18th century CE
Tempera on paper
Acc no – 49. 19/129

This painting illustrates the Prakasa Samyoga, that Kesavadasa describes as 'love that is manifested or realised, when one sees its reflection in the mirror'. Keshvadasa writes of the divine couple who were seated on the couch, engrossed in love, when Krishna reflects on the beauty of Radha in the mirror.

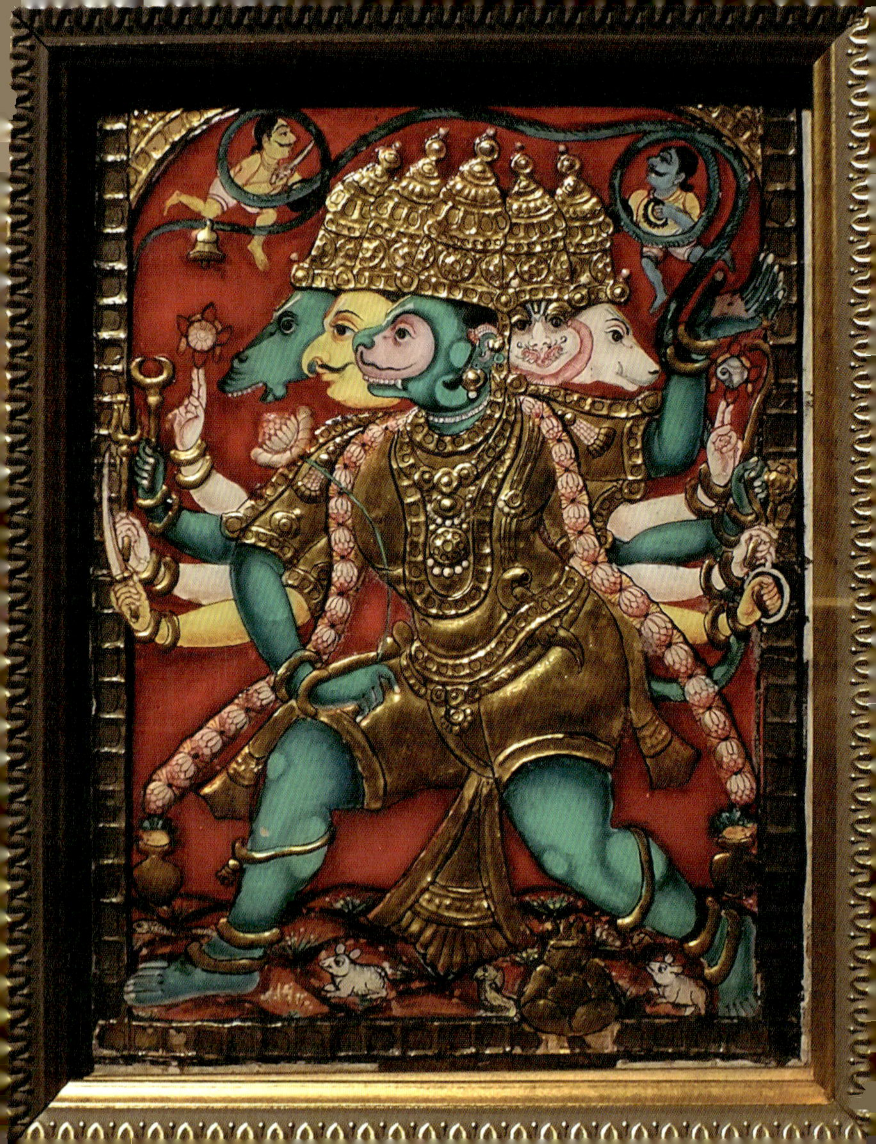

Panchmukhi Hanuman
Early 19th century CE
Cloth pasted on wood
Acc no – 62.910

Panchmukhi or the five-faced aspect of Hanuman can be traced to the Ramayana, where Hanuman takes on five incarnations as Hanuman, Narsimha, Varaha, Hayagriva and Garuda to extinguish five lamps in five different directions at the same time or to kill Mahiravan, the King of Patla. The five directions are Garuda as West, Narsimha as South, Varaha as North, Hanuman as East and Hayagriva as *Akasha*, the sky.

ANTHROPOLOGY

The collection at the National Museum in the Anthropology section, consists of nearly 10,000 artefacts. To build this collection, the participation of private donors as well as many forays into tribal and rural areas, were imperative. This collection has textiles, terracottas, paintings and wood carvings, a range of different headgear, footwear, dresses, ornaments, musical instruments, scrolls, masks, weapons, metal images, leather puppets and more.

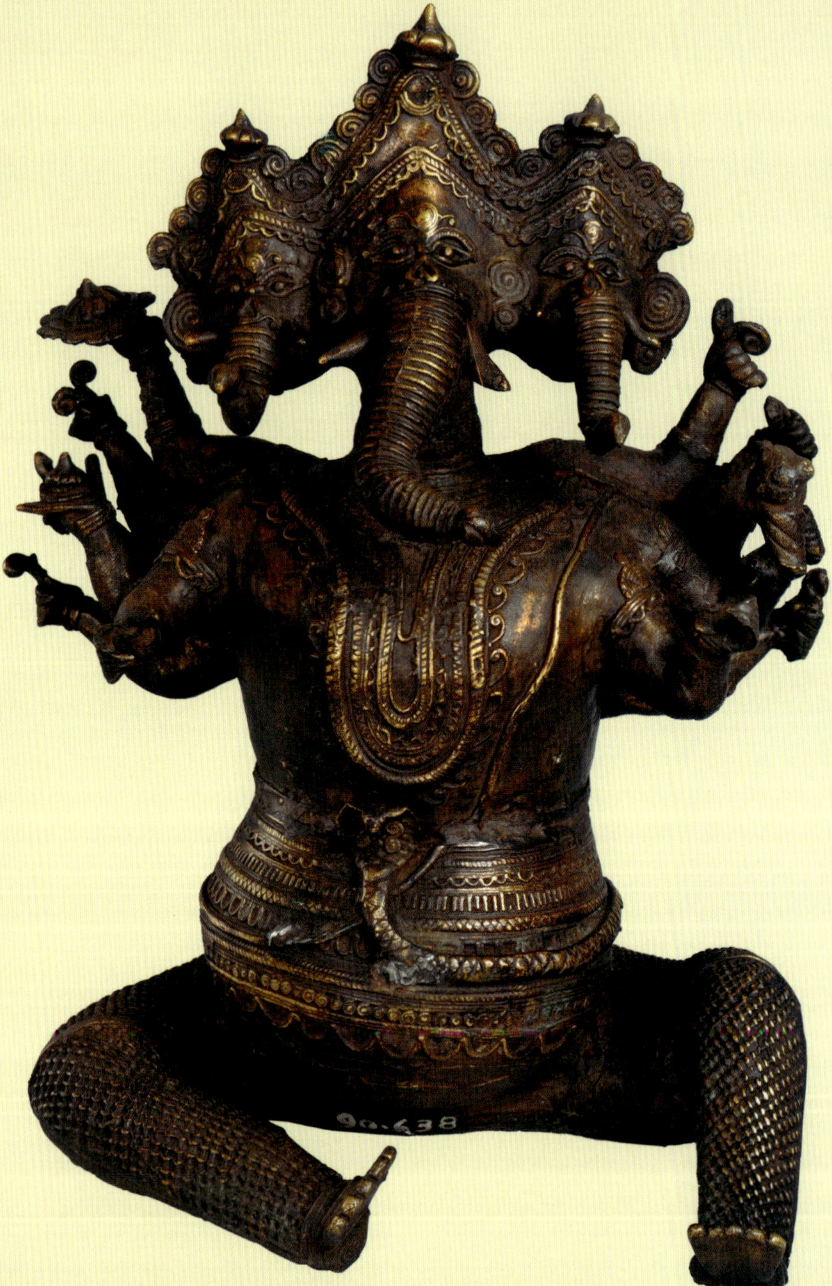
90.638

ANTHROPOLOGY

Ganesh
20th century
Bronze
Acc no – 90.638

Ganesh is one of the most iconic and popular gods of the Hindu pantheon. His name Ganesh or Ganapati suggests he is the lord of the *ganas* (dwarfs attendants of Siva), although he is popularly worshipped as Vighnesha (the lord of obstacles) and Siddhidata (the bestower of success). Before the start of any act in life, whether it is religious, academic, cultural, social or commercial, he is evoked in prayers to remove all obstacles and help in achieving success. In the bronze images from Bastar, he is often shown as a king riding an elephant or is represented with multiple faces.

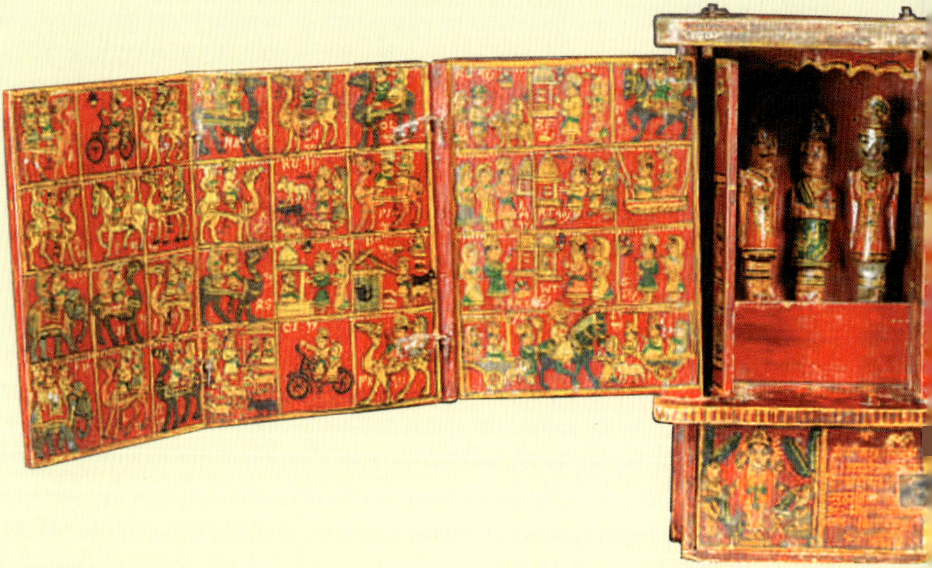

ANTHROPOLOGY

Kavad (Portable Shrine)
20th century
Wood, metal; painted, carved
Acc no 24.524

A *kavad* is a portable shrine, which contains multiple folding doors, each painted with various themes from the Hindu epics and mythology. It is a folk tradition from the state of Rajasthan, where the Kavadia or Bhatt priests commission the artisans belonging to the Kumawat caste to create these delightful portable shrines.

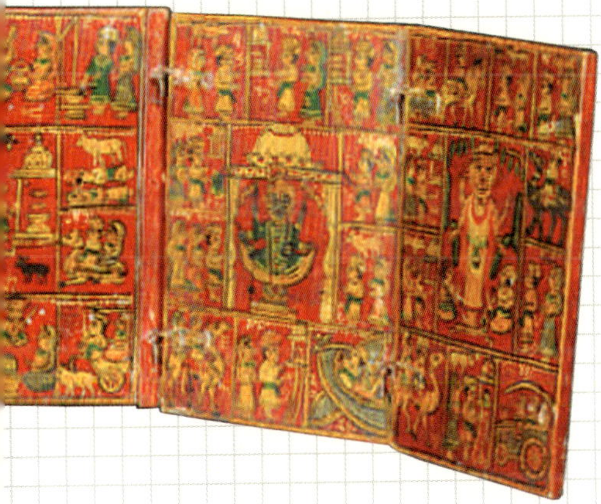

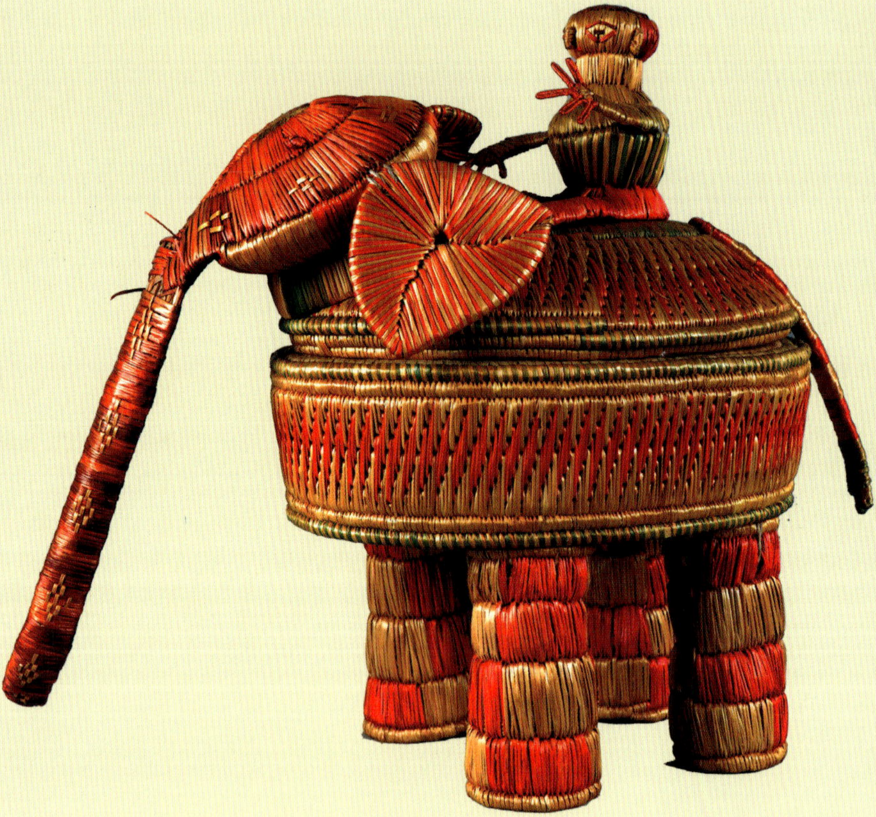

ANTHROPOLOGY

Elephant
20th century
Sikki grass
Acc no – 71.673

The craft of basketry gives the craftsmen flexibility to play with the forms and create works of art by just exploiting the various shades of strips in their weaving pattern. For example, the elephant-shaped *sikki* grass basket from Bihar is a fine example of creativity, where the dyed grass is coiled along with the natural coloured grass, to make an object distinct to the region and its aesthetics.

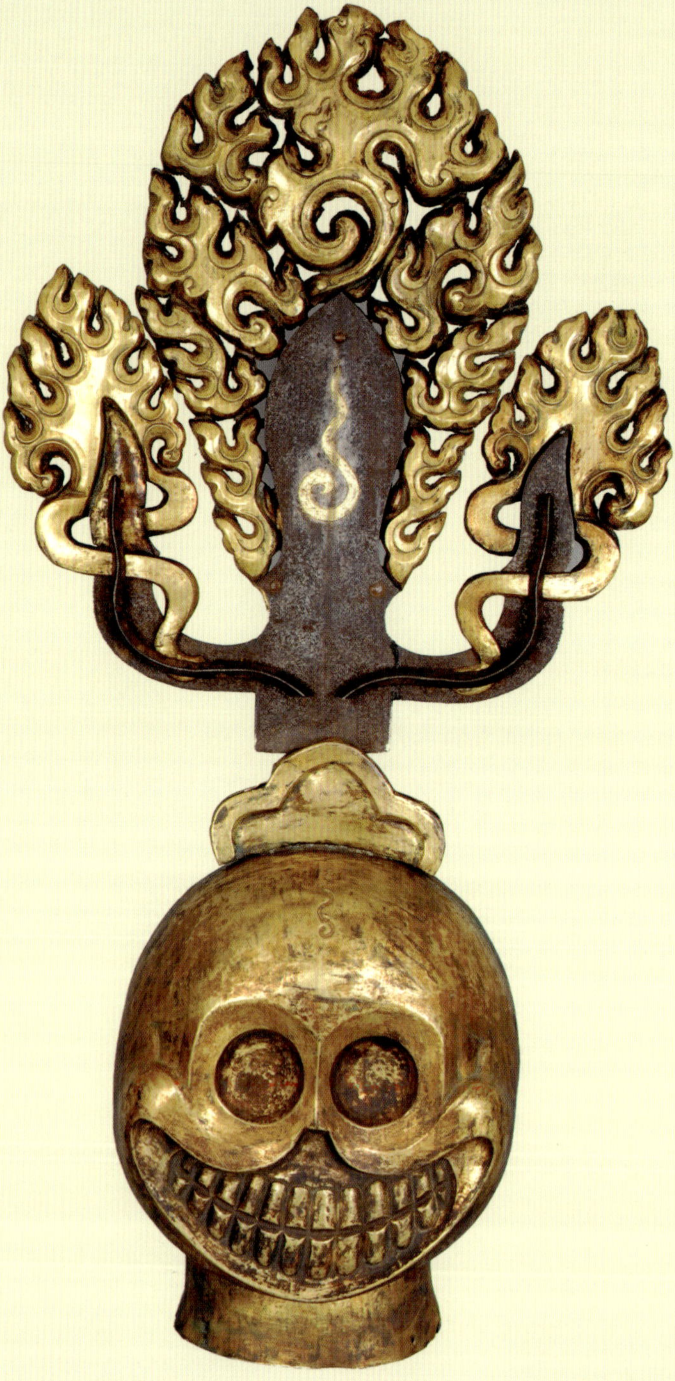

ANTHROPOLOGY

The Lord of Soil (Sadbag)
Early 20th century CE
Metal
Acc no – 91.139

This is a ritual image of 'Sabdag'—the local guardian deity of the mountains manifesting a large gold plated metallic skull and a detachable trident of iron, depicting blazing flames. The skull represents the ferocious form of Lord Siva, that is Bhairava. It is marked with a cranial suture and has a slit at the apex to fix the trident. The trident and the flames are symbolic of the energy in Lord Siva. These iconic images can be seen on the rooftops of monasteries, securing protection against evil spirits and demons that are believed to pollute the earth, air and water. They also ward off all evil from the holy site.

COINS

From the the 1st millennium BCE, coins of India were made of copper and silver. Evidence points to the fact that metal currency was minted in India well before the period of the Mauryan Empire. Punch marked coins were issued between the 6th century BCE and the 1st century CE.

For the sheer variety, aesthetic sensitivity and rich narrative content, the Gupta gold coins remain unsurpassed. Those gold coins also commemorate socio-political events such as marriage alliances (king-and-queen coin during the reign of Chandragupta I) and the artistic and personal accomplishments of royalty. Originality and fine skill characterise Mughal coins, which rank amongst the greatest in the world. The Ilahi coins of Akbar recorded the religious ideals cherished by the emperor.

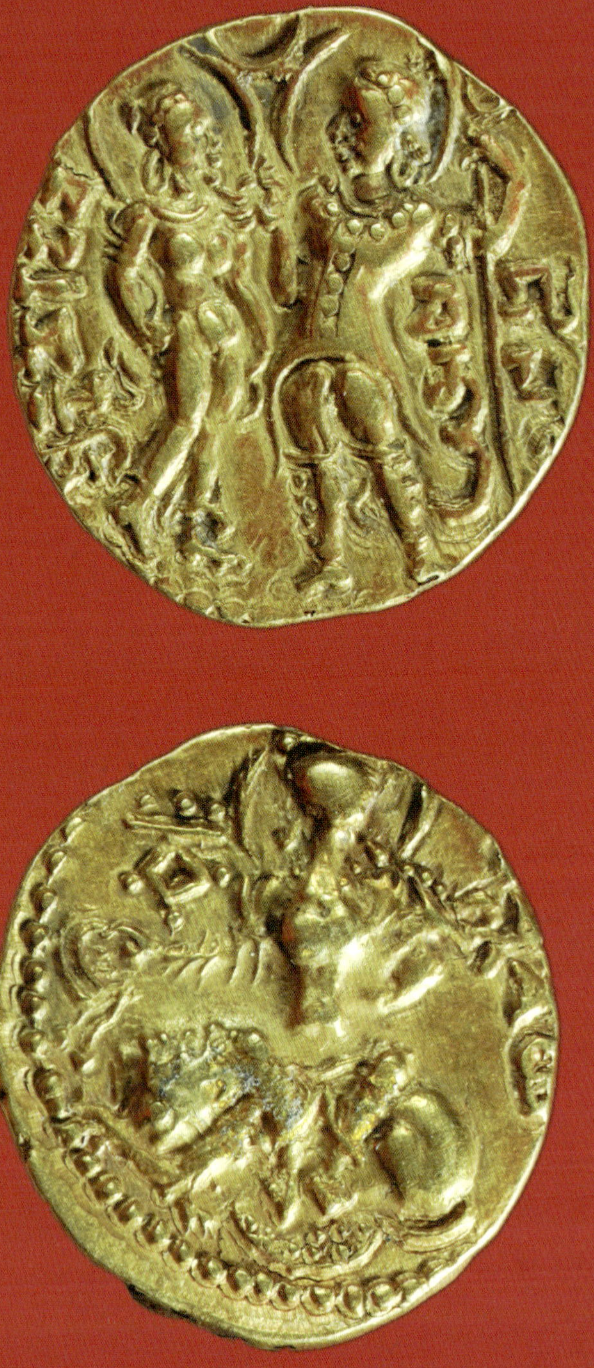

Gupta
326-330 CE
Gold
Acc no – 51.50/1

King and Queen—the King is offering a bangle like object to the Queen; name of the king in Brahmi—Chandragupta (right); name of the queen in Brahmi—Sri Kumaradevi (left).

The Goddess Durga is seated on a lion, holding a noose and a cornucopia.

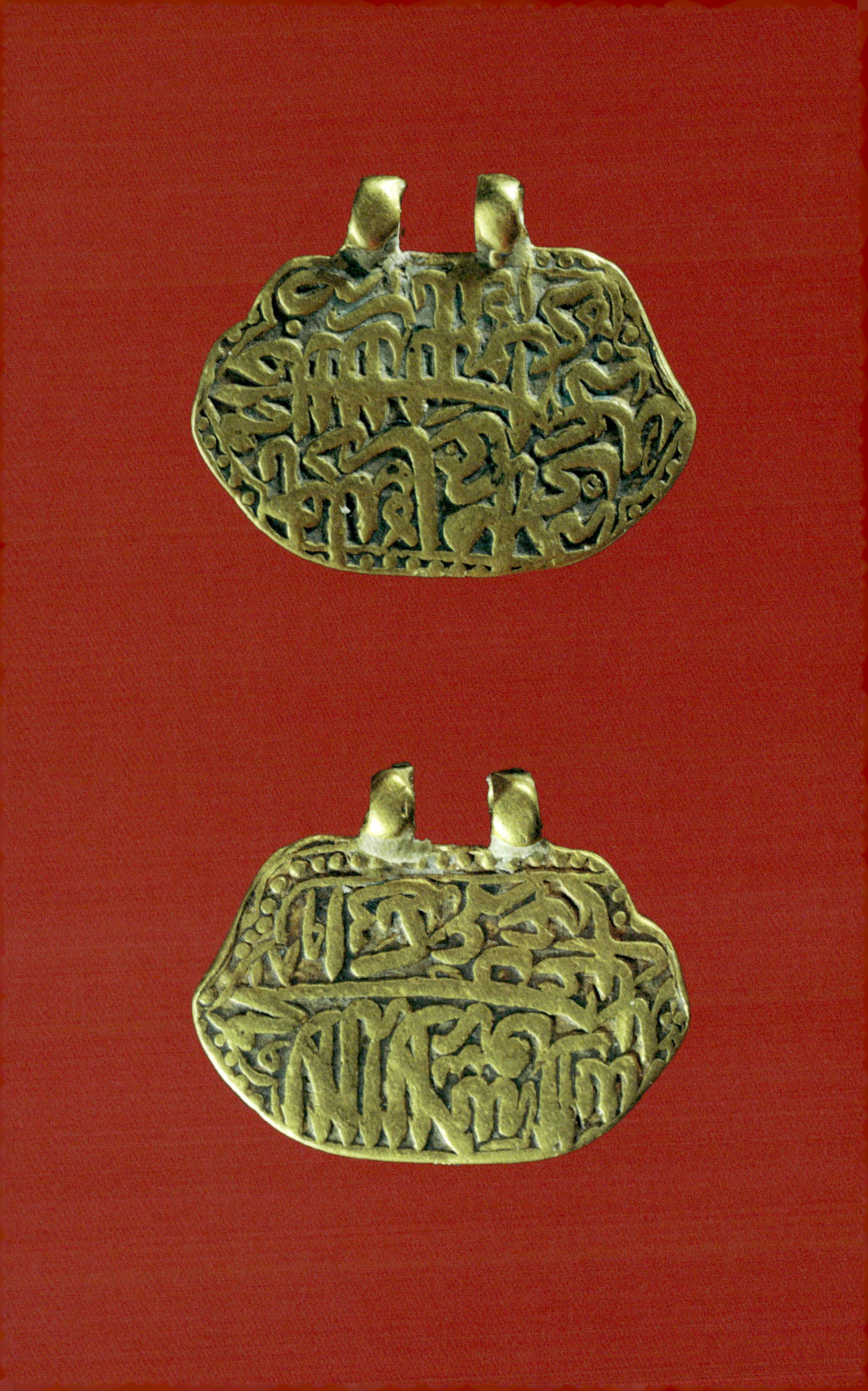

COINS

Mughal
1556-1605 CE (963-1014 AH)
Gold
Acc no - . 60.1165/3546

Jalaluddin Muhammad Akbar 1556-1605 CE (963-1014 AH).
Gold Mehrabi 10.8 gm. 2.4 x 3.1 cm. Agra. In the centre: Kalima; name of four caliphs, date 981 AH.
In the centre: Jalal-al-din Muhammad Akbar Badshah Ghazi, above: khallad Mulkahu, below - Zarb Baladah Agra.

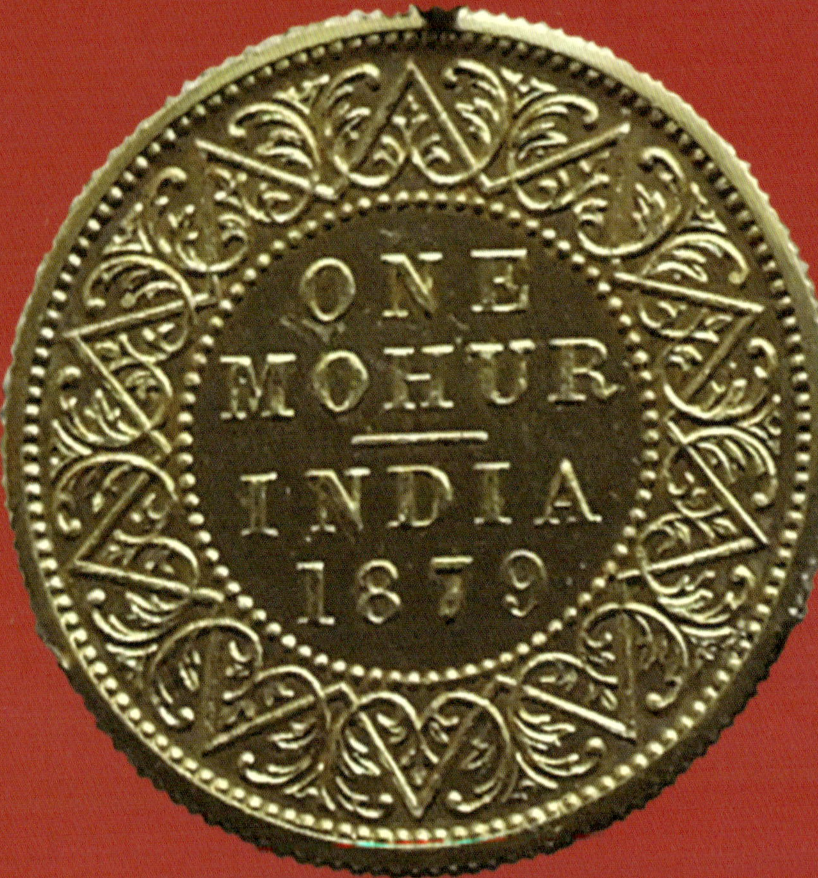
ONE
MOHUR
INDIA
1879

COINS

Indo-British
19th century CE
Gold
Acc no - 86.346/8

Empress Victoria 19th Century CE. Mohur Gold 3.4 gm Dia: 2.6 cm; W: 11.4 cm. Centre—Bust of Queen to left, Inscription: Left—Victoria, Right—Empress. Within decorated border denomination and date in the Centre–"One Mohur India 1879".

MANUSCRIPTS

A vast number of manuscripts, in various languages and scripts, spanning a range of subjects have been acquired and restored to keep alive past chronicles. Some of these manuscripts are illustrated and some are not. Several are embellished with real gold foil. The illustrations embody miniature styles of art as practised in different parts of India through the different ages.

The collection at the National Museum covers a period of more than 1,200 years, from the 7th to 19th century. These are on parchment, palm leaves, birch bark, paper, cloth and copper plates. The incomplete text from the *Quran* (7th century CE), *Ashtasahasrika Prajnaparmita* (12th century), *Bal Bodhini* (2nd century) and *Shahnama* (1830 CE) are few of the treasures in this splendid collection.

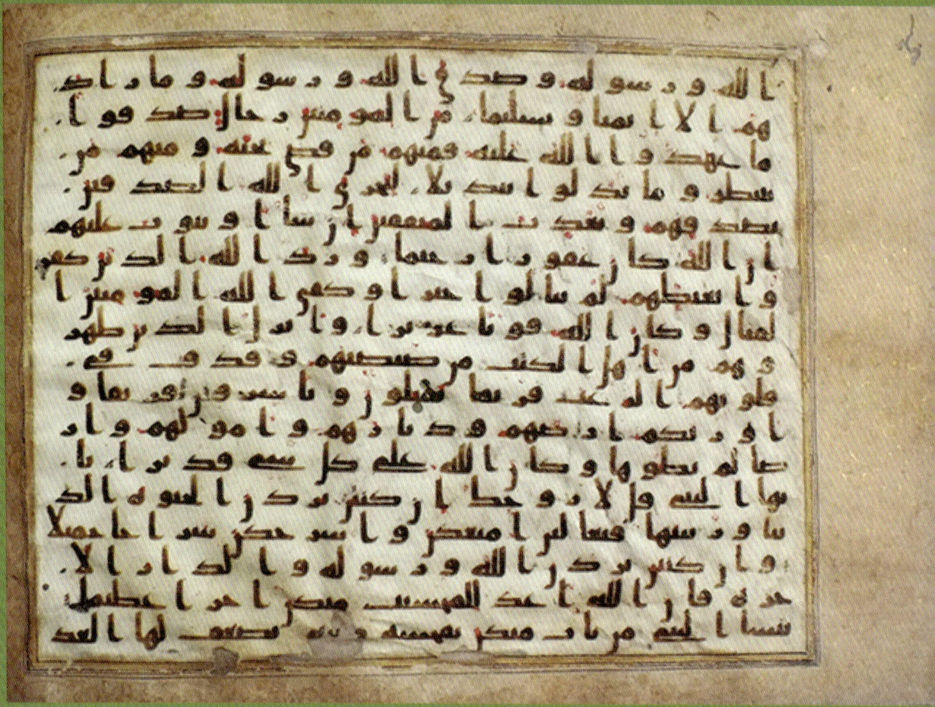

MANUSCRIPTS

Holy Quran
7th century CE
Parchment
Acc no - 56.62/4.

This is an incomplete text from the Holy Quran (7th Century CE) inscribed by Hazrat Ali, the fourth Caliph of Islam. It is on parchment (untanned animal skin) and seems to be restored with a 16th century paper bearing Persian inscriptions. It is a rare specimen of both text and calligraphy.

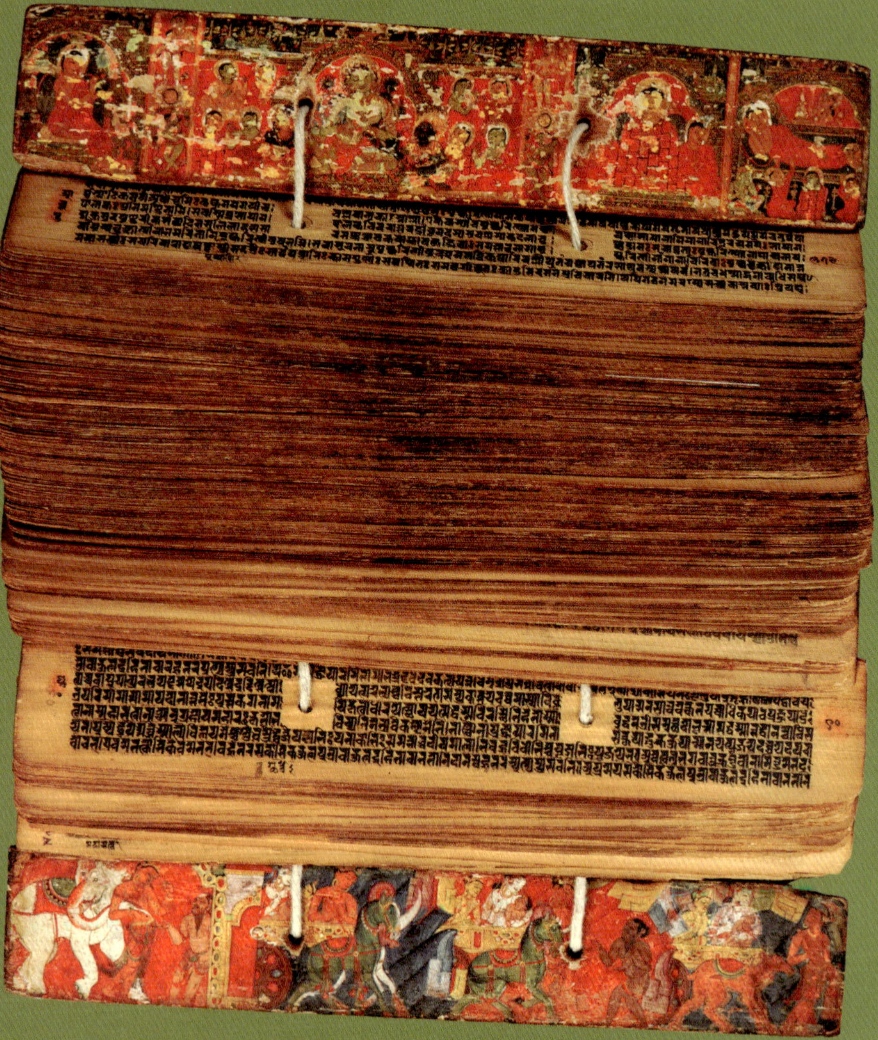

MANUSCRIPTS

Astasahasrika Prajnaparamita
12th century CE
Palm leaf
Acc no - 51.212

The Mahayana philosophy of Budhhism is encapsulated in these Prajnaparamitas. The *Asthasahasrika Prajnaparamita* comprises 8,000 units, each with 32 syllables. Its *shlokas* (hymns) are written in the form of a dialogue between Buddha and two of his disciples, Shariputra and Subhuti, with the latter posing questions and the former answering them. The six Paramitas in Mahayana Buddhism were written to attain supreme knowledge, and for a Bodhisattva (a deity from the Buddhist pantheon who delays his enlightenment to help others to be enlightened) to attain Buddhahood.

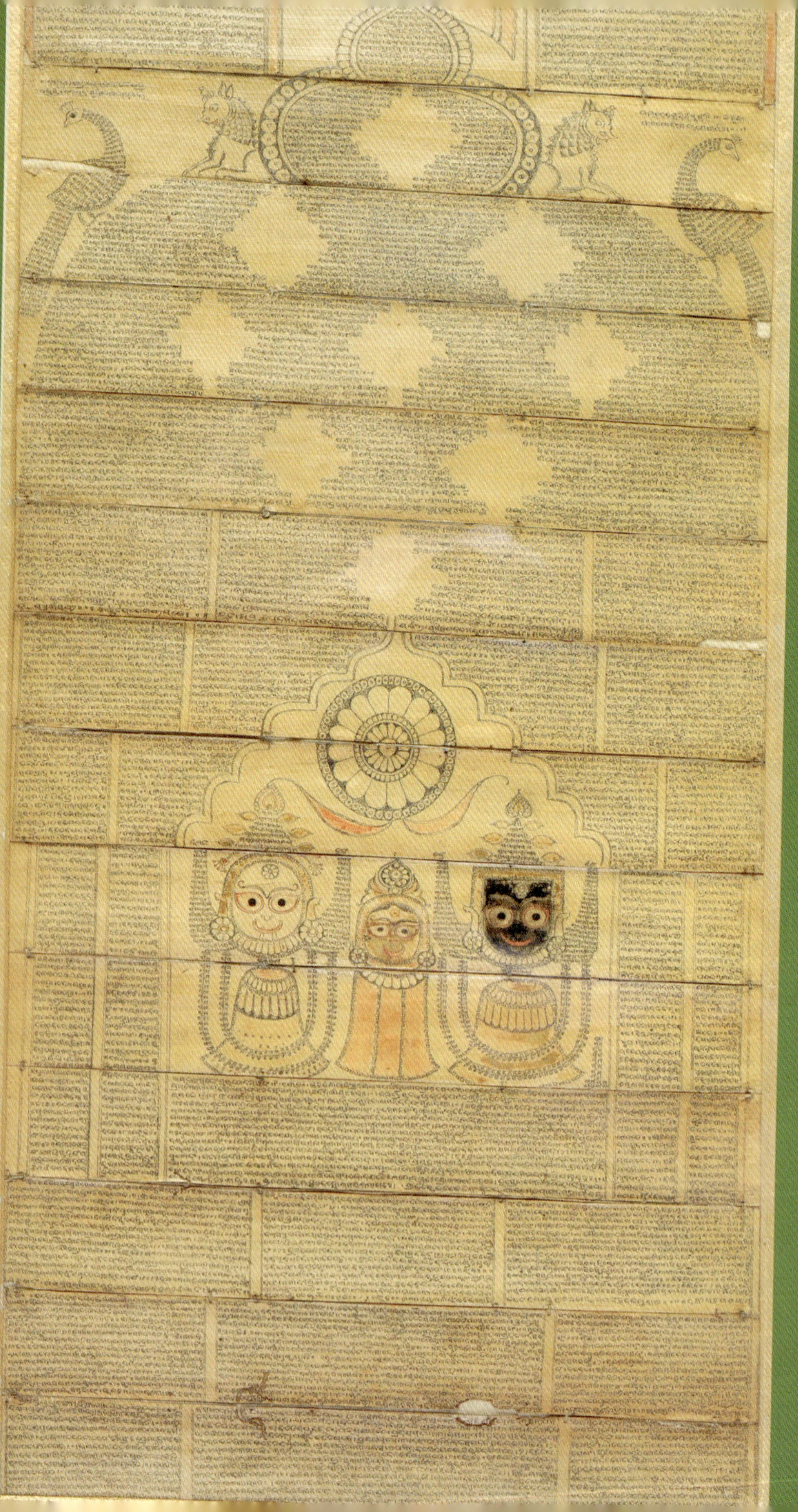

MANUSCRIPTS

Gita Govinda
18th century CE
Palm leaf
Acc no - 57.46

Fourteen palm-leaves have been stitched together to open like a hanging and contain Jayadeva's great lyrical poem to Krishna—the 'Love Song of the Dark Lord' or *Gita Govinda*. Radha commands her divine lover to paint a leaf on her breasts, 'put colour on my cheeks, lay a girdle on my hips, twine my heavy braid with flowers, fix rows of bangles on my hands, and put jewelled anklets on my feet' with all doubts resolved. An eager Krishna, 'does what Radha asked'. There is a central image on this hanging. The text is so artfully written that the arrangement of words creates the outline of the Jagannath Puri temple façade. At the top of the temple spire are sculpted lions and peacocks and a flag fluttering in the wind, these forms are filled with minutely written Sanskrit verses.

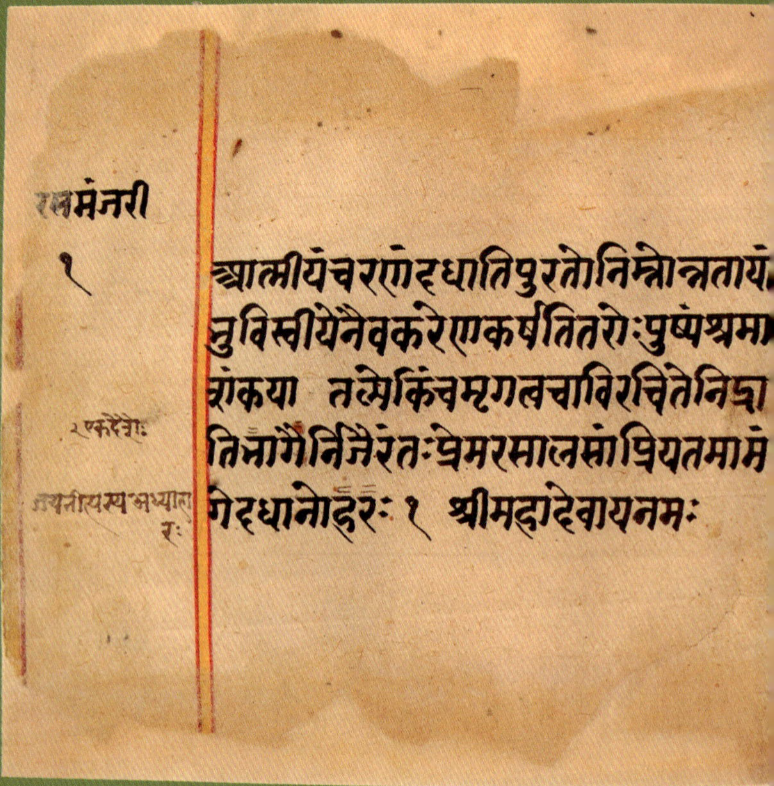

रसमंजरी
१
२ एकदेशेन:
नयनीयस्य अध्याहारः

आत्मीयं चरणं दधाति पुरतो निम्नोन्नतायां
भुवि स्वीयेनैव करेण कर्षति ततो रोः पुष्पश्रमा
शंकया तल्पे किंच मृगत्वचा विरचिते निद्रा
ति भागैर्निजैरंतः प्रेमरसालसां प्रियतमामं
गे दधानो हरः १ श्रीमद्गणेशाय नमः

MANUSCRIPTS

Rasamanjari
18th century CE
Paper
Acc no - 61.1185

One of the great classics of Sanskrit literature is Bhanudatta's 15th century work, *Rasamanjari*. This first folio contains an invocatory verse in honour of Siva. The deity in the role of a lover is portrayed in the Ardhanarishwara form, the 'Lord whose half is Woman'. The text says. "Siva looks at the uneven ground, hesitates, then extends his right foot. Roaming about in the forest, he plucks wild flowers. Relaxing in comfort on his bed [covered with] a tiger's pelt, he presses his beloved to his body's side...' Everything points to Siva trying to save his beloved, his left female half which is Parvati.

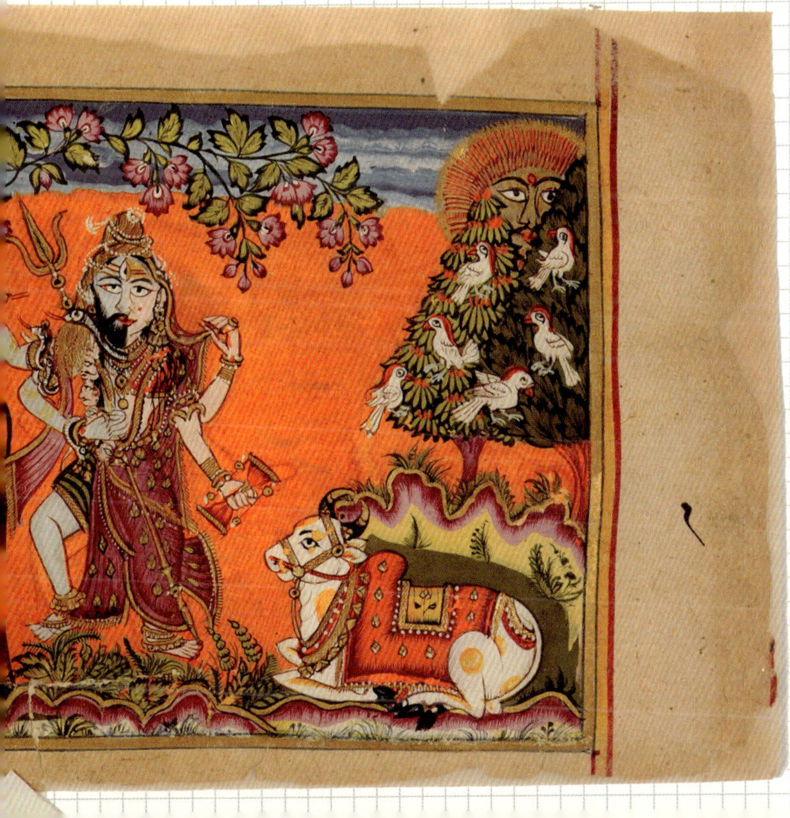

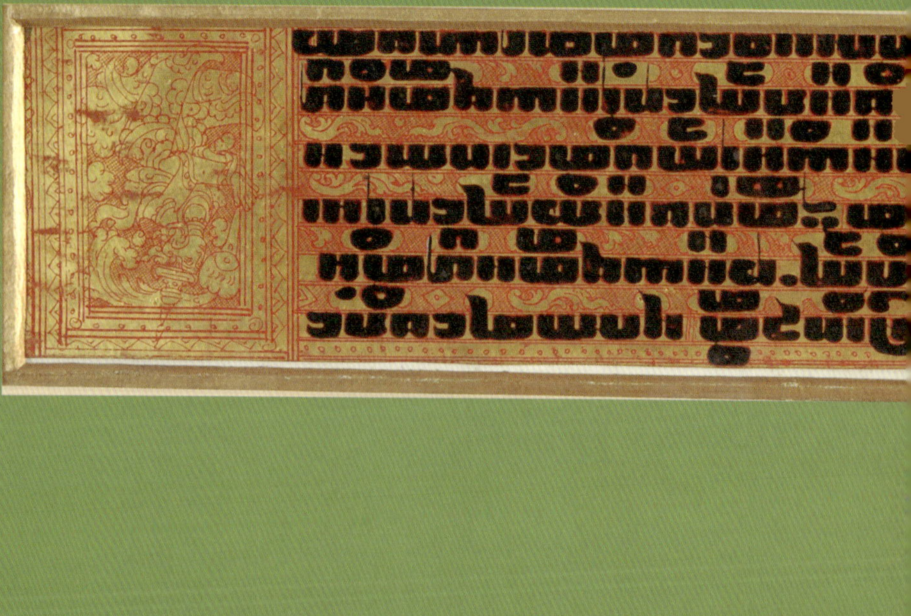

Kamnavacha

19th century CE
Metal (smeared with gold)
Acc no - 51.20

Kamnavacha are among the most sacred of Burmese religious texts. They consist of nine *khandakas* (sections) from the Pali Vinaya Pitaka, each of which relates to a specific ceremony associated with the monks of the Theravada school of Buddhism. Kamnavacha were usually commissioned as works of merit to be presented to the monkhood when a son entered the Buddhist order as a novice or became ordained as a monk.

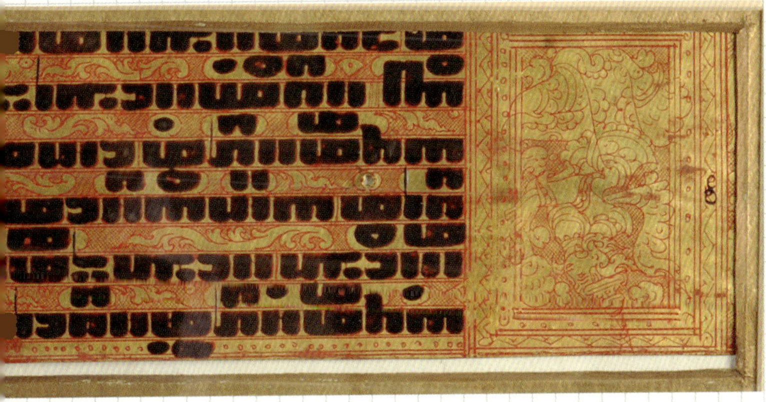

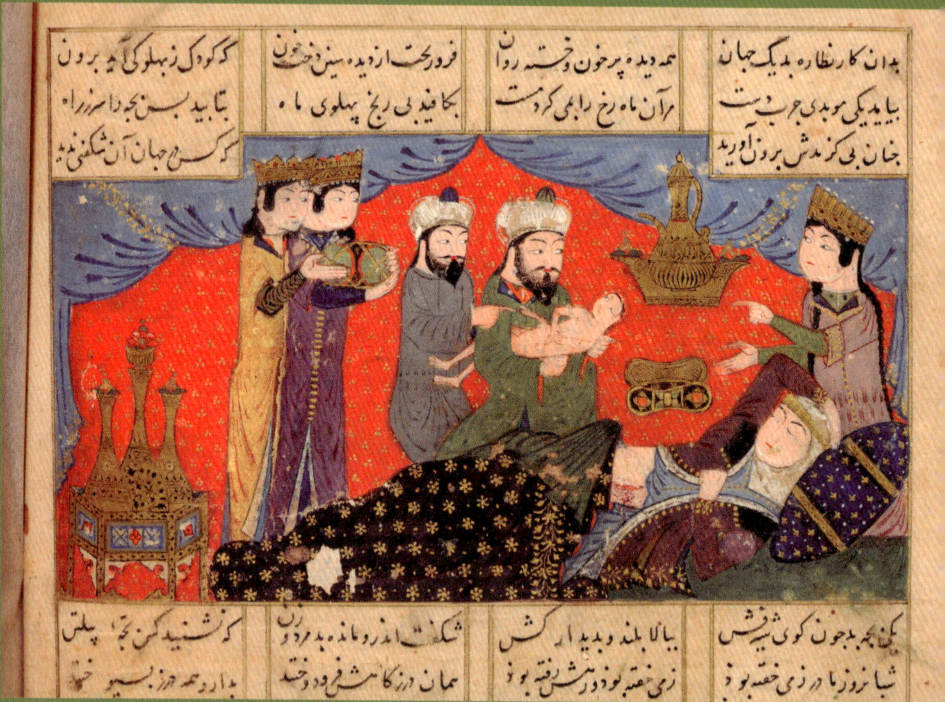

Shahnama
1830 CE
Paper
Acc no - 53.2/8

Shahnama is a great Persian epic authored by Abu'l Qasim Firdausi Tusi (935–1020 CE) in 1010 CE and translated by Malik Sharif-al-Din-al-Qadri. It chronicles the lives and times of 50 kings of Persia in 50 chapters. This copy of *Shahanama* was written and illustrated in Lahore in 1830 and has numerous beautiful illustrations. The *Shahnama* tells the tales of heroic deeds, achievements, love, power and valour of the 50 kings of Persia. It has nearly 50,000 rhyming couplets.

DECORATIVE ARTS

Decorative arts relate to the design, form and embellishment of objects of utility. Every culture has its distinct features that are clearly reflected in the fine craftsmanship, ranging from surface tiles and wood carvings, ceramic and metal utensils to textiles and jewellery. These functional objects help us comprehend the social, religious, economical, commercial and technological realities of a particular society.

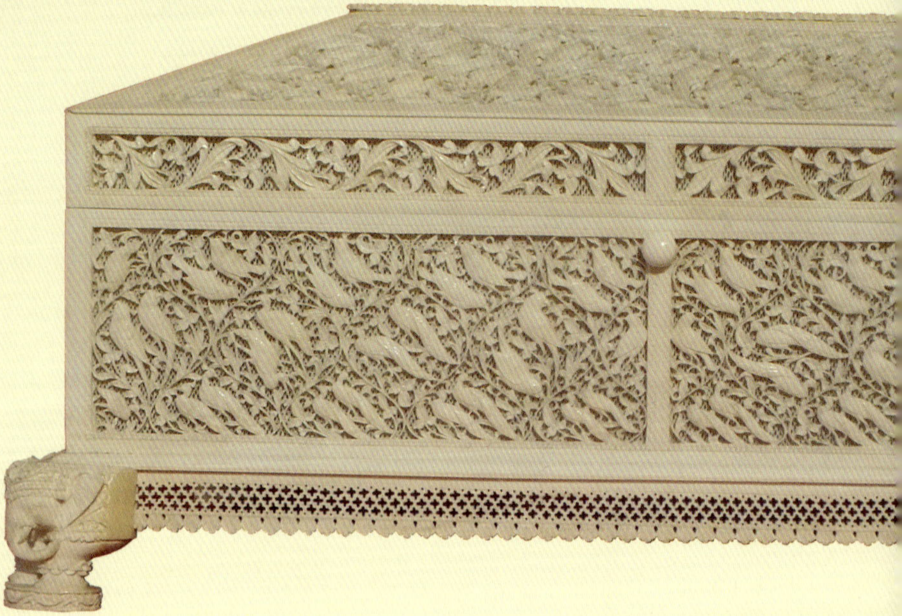

Jewellery Box

20th century CE
Ivory; carved
Acc no – 90.347

Intricate *jaali* (lattice) work is the most significant feature of the Mughal monuments of India. This minutely carved ivory jewellery box is an excellent example of lattice workmanship done by the Delhi ivory carvers in the beginning of the 20th century. Fitted with several delicate small panels, worked in ogee pattern, where each ogee design shows symmetrically arranged pair of birds.

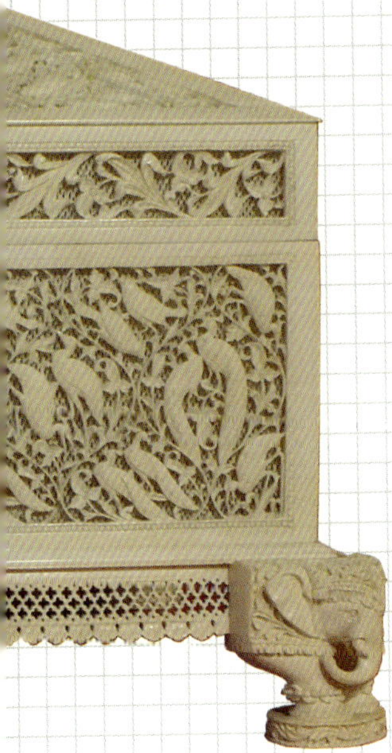

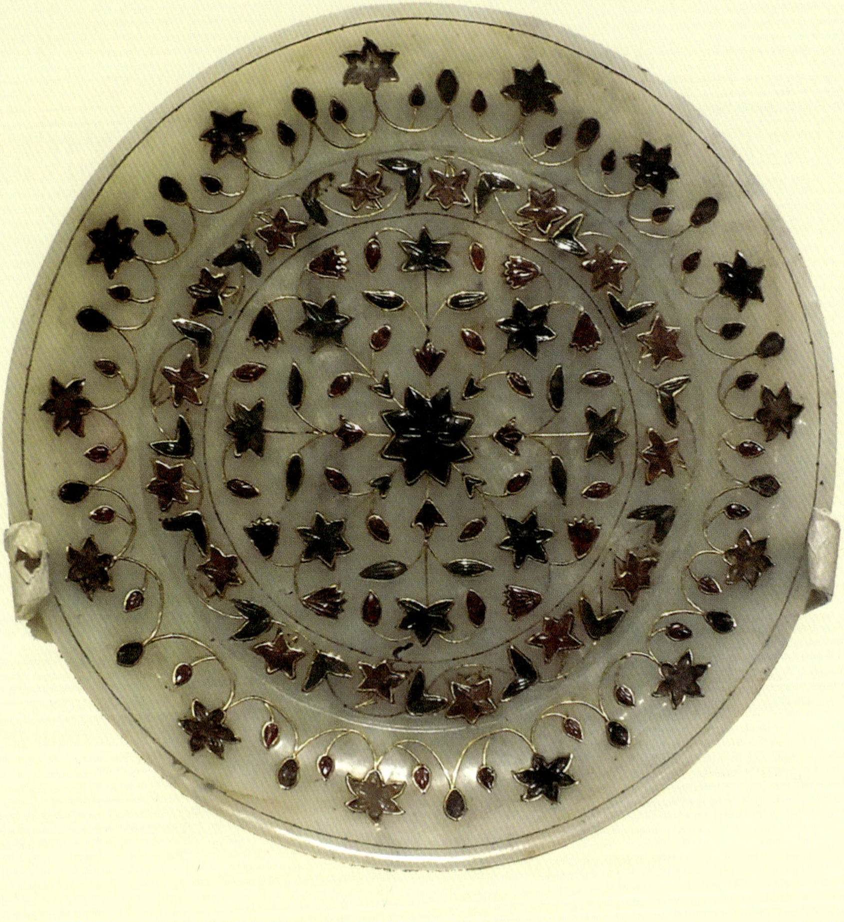

DECORATIVE ARTS AND WOODEN ARTEFACTS

Plate

18th century CE

Jade; inlaid with precious stones and gold wire

Acc no – 48.9/1

This plate made up of jade and immaculately inlaid with precious stones and gold wire shows the skill involved in delicately inlaying simple utilitarian objects. Jade has been used in many countries as a popular medium for decorative arts as it has an internal quality of being translucent and allowing light to pass through it.

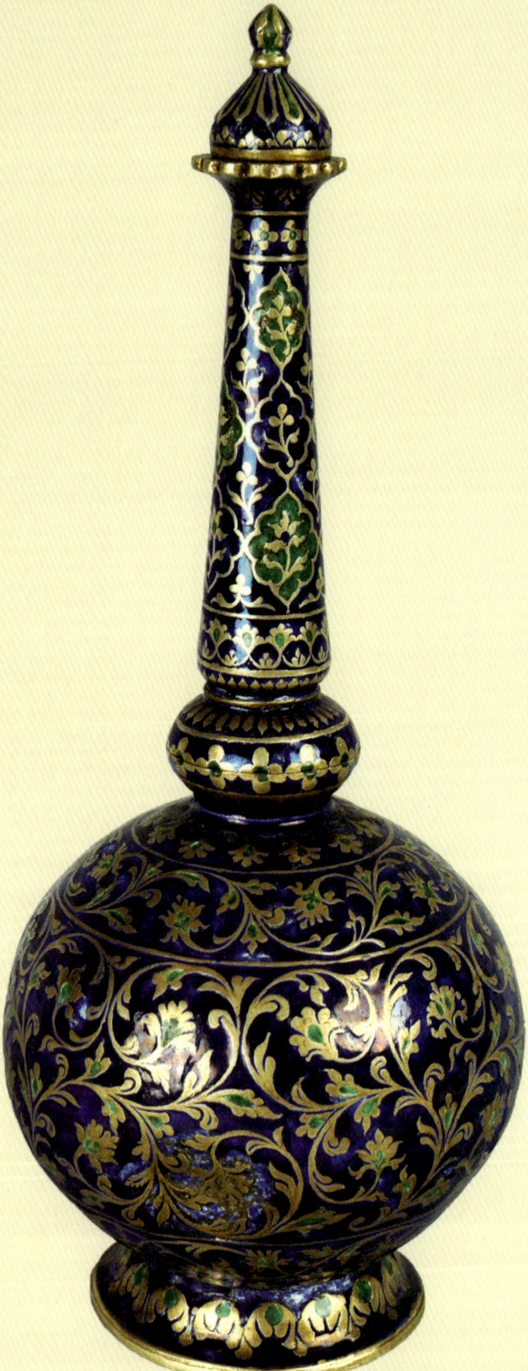

Rose water sprinkler
Late 18th century CE
Silver; enamelled
Acc no – 91.120

This silver and gilded enamelled *gulabpash* has a bulbous body for storing rose water, a little circular base and a long neck. The beautiful *gulabpash* is decorated with the Champleve technique of enamelling in blue and green.

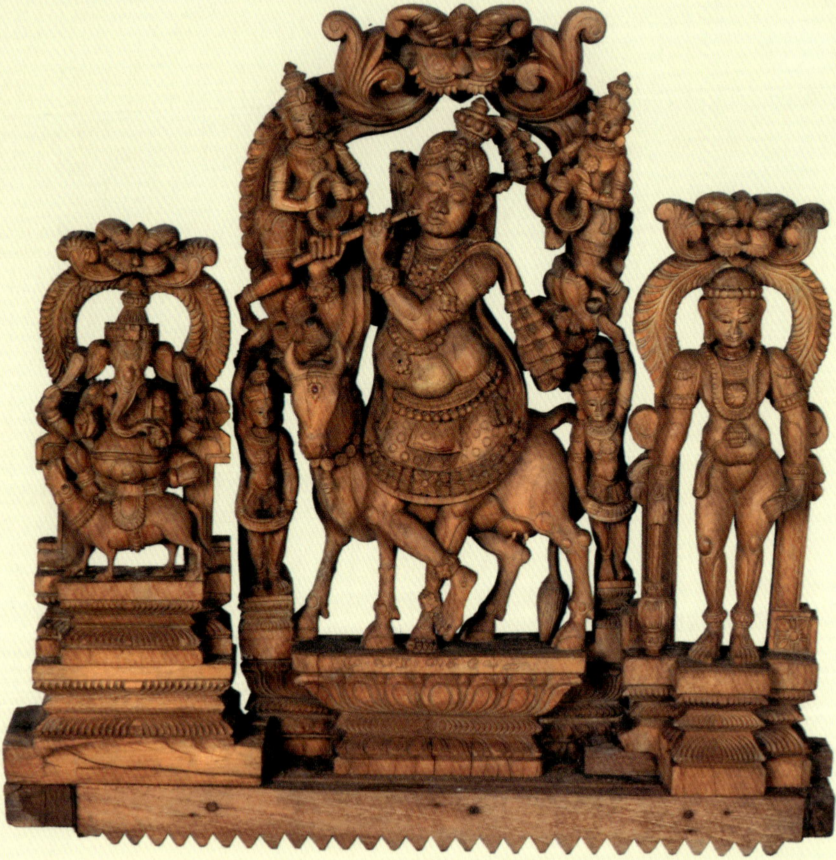

Venugopal, Ganesha and Saint

19th century CE

Wood

Acc no – 62.103

The intricately carved statue of Venugopal in the centre is flanked by Ganesha and images of saint on both sides and all of them stand on a lotus seat. All three divinities stand under a carved arch, which depicts *Kirtimukha* (face of glory) on top, and their seats have been fixed on a long rectangular pedestal.

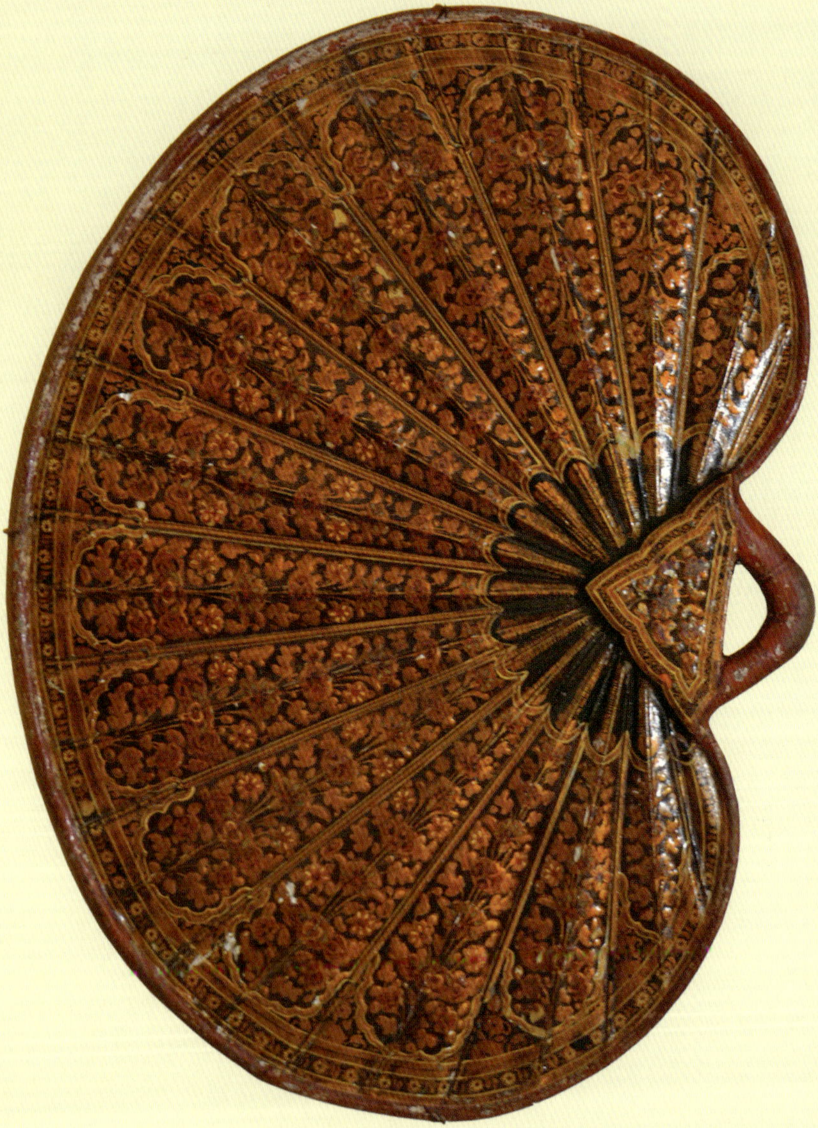

DECORATIVE ARTS AND WOODEN ARTEFACTS

Fan

Late 19th century CE

Palm leaf, wood, cloth (cotton)

Acc no – 64.466

The palm leaf's natural stems form the basic structure of this fan, which has been covered with fine muslin. On this smooth surface, the painting has been done with the 'gesso technique'. After the painting is done on the smooth surface, the patterns are painted with natural pigments and the fan beautifully illustrates the floral motifs on one side and peacock feather-like motifs on the other.

ARMS AND ARMOUR

One can trace the evolution of mankind through the arms and armour that was used at different times. From primitive, crude stone weapons to fight wild animals, to the discovery of metal, which facilitated the crafting of sophisticated and more advanced innovations, arms and armour reflect their times.

Most of these pieces belong to heroes of the past. The inscribed bow of Bahadur Shah II, the Flintcock Gun, the inscribed axe of Nadir Shah, the shield of Maharana Sangram Singh II, all deserve special mention.

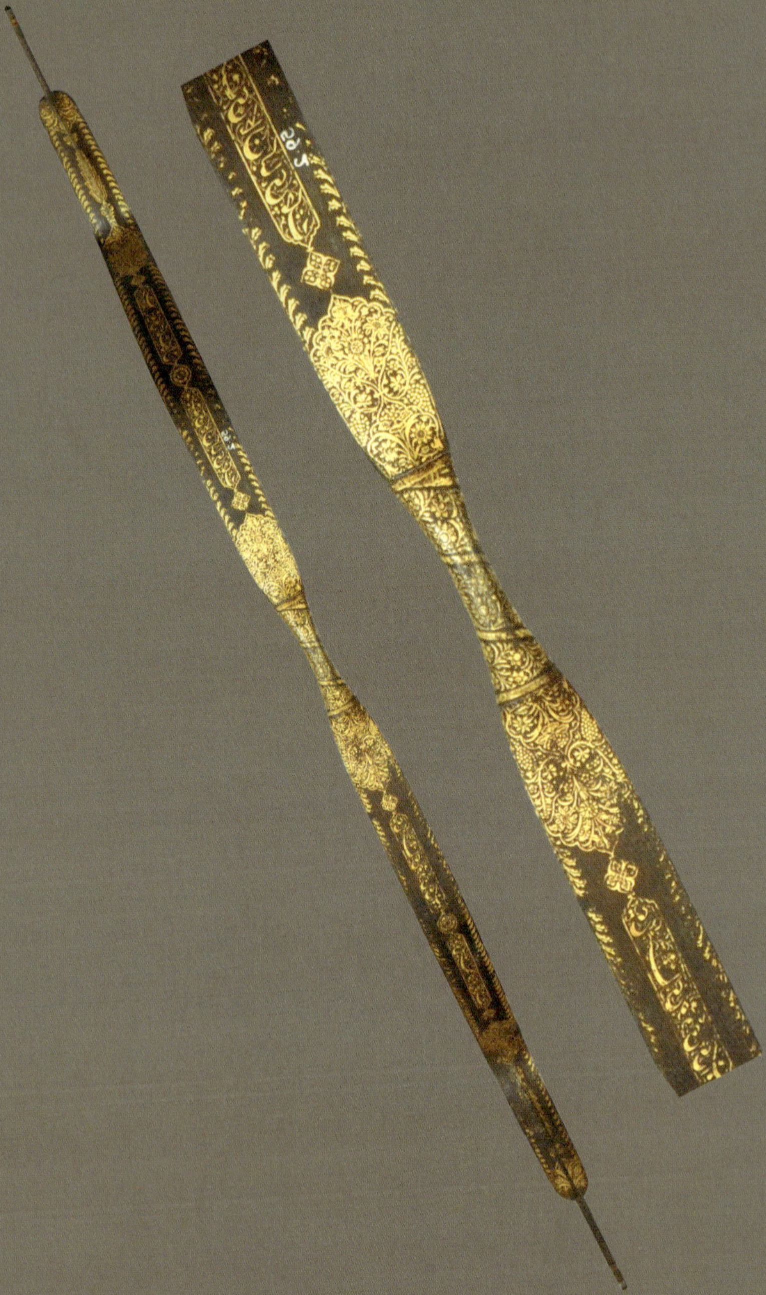

Inscribed Bow of Bahadur Shah II
c.1850 CE
Steel
Acc no - 59.2

This is a triple-curved bow made of fine steel belonging to Bahadur Shah II, the last ruler of the Mughal dynasty, with his name and couplets inscribed in Urdu. The bow is beautifully damascened all over in gold and is without a string.

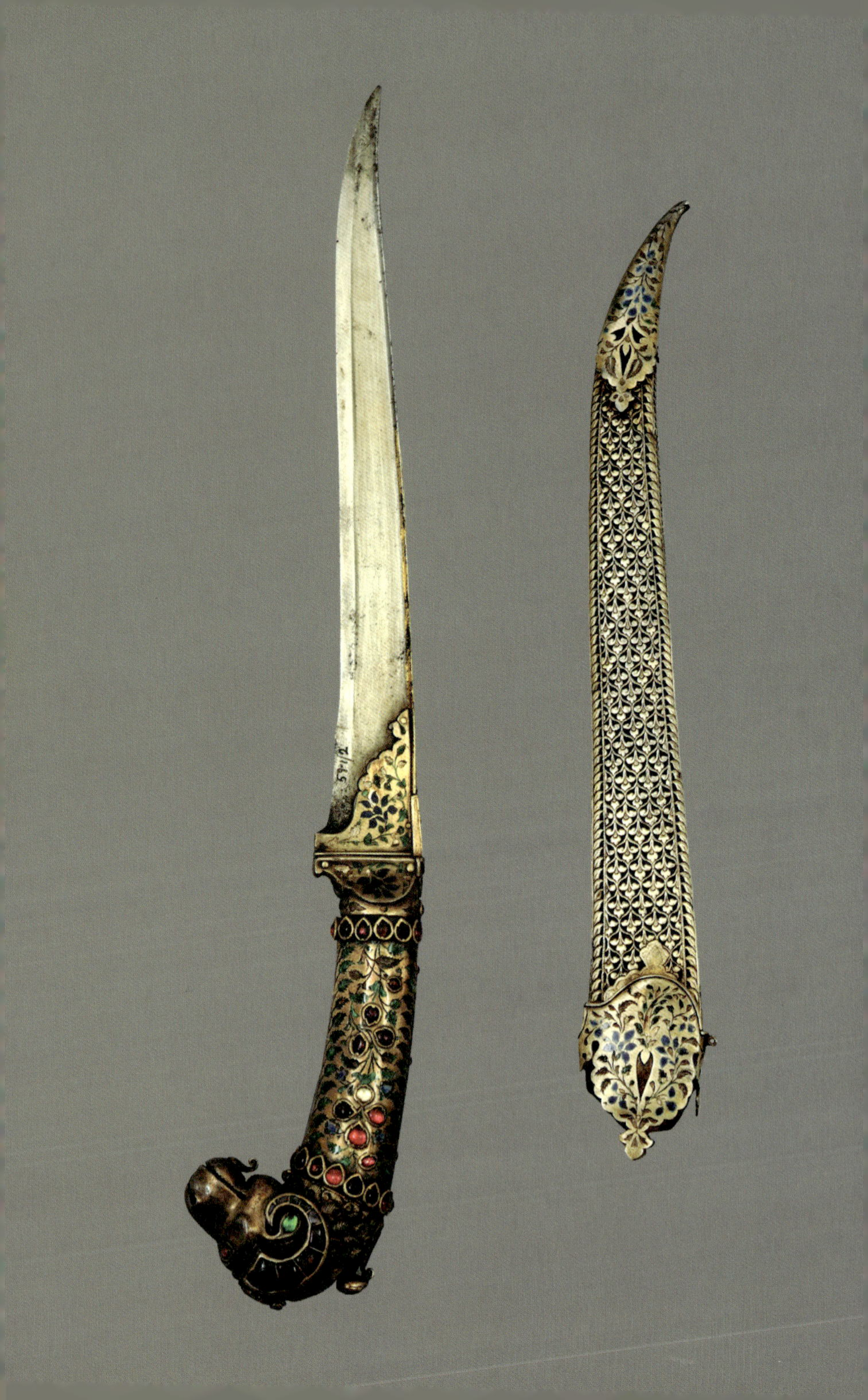

Enamelled Dagger
Late 17th century CE
Steel, ivory, wood
Acc no - 59.1/2

This is a straight-bladed dagger with a straight hilt and no guard. The blade tapers gradually and the hilt is thin, slender and delicate. It is similar to a *peshqabz* (a variant of dagger) but while the latter is a sturdy weapon, the *kard* is a fanciful specimen generally carried by the queen or the princess. The *kard*, in question, has a single edged blade of Damascus steel whose point is thickened to permit it to be passed through metal, if needed. The ram-shaped hilt of metal is profusely encrusted with rubies, emeralds and other jewels. The sheath of metal is delicately perforated with images of gods and goddesses.

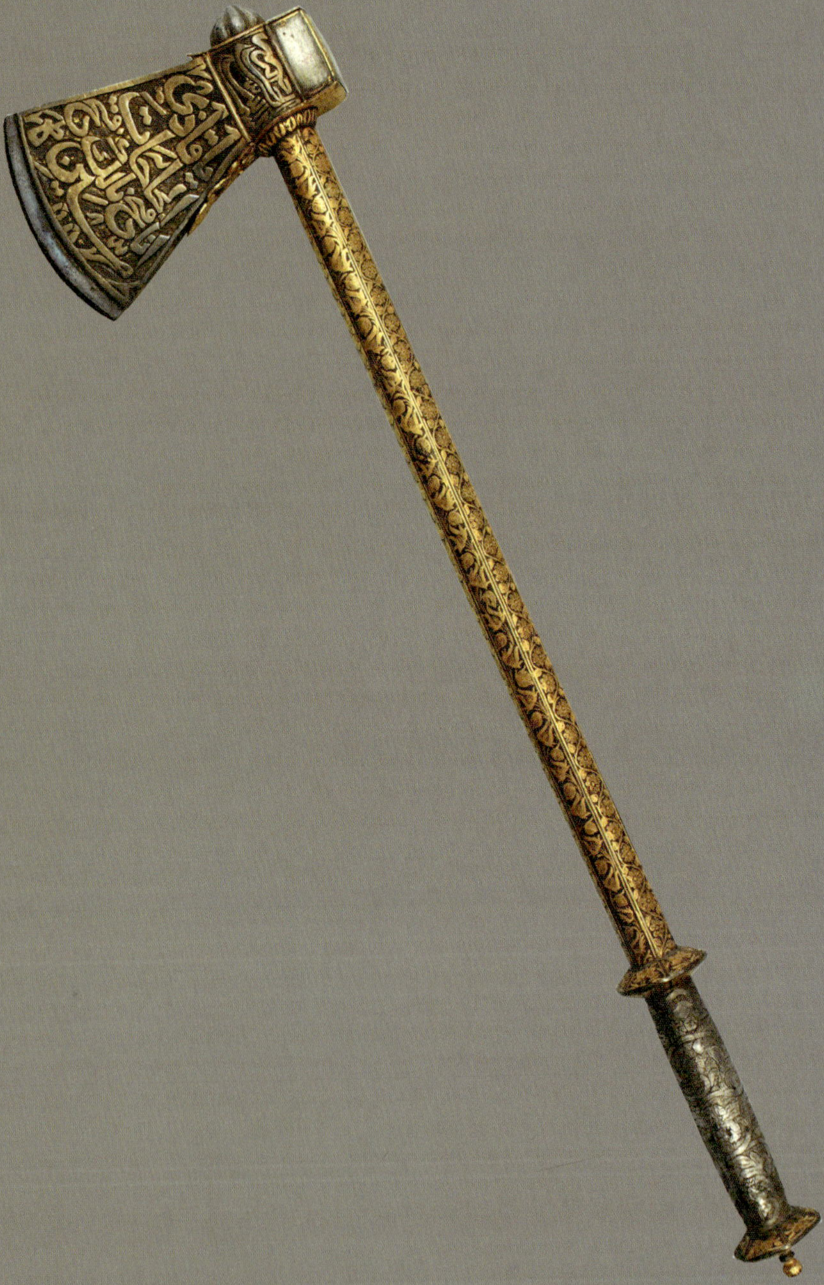

Inscribed Battle Axe of Nadir Shah
c. 1739 CE
Steel
Acc no - 58.47/3

A personal battle axe of Nadir Shah who invaded India and Delhi in 1739 CE. It is inscribed with verses from the Holy Quran, and Nadir Shah's name and the title Sahib-i-Qiran. There are only three Sahib-i-Qirans in Mughal history: Timur, Shah Jahan and Nadir Shah. The inscription engraved in high relief on both sides of the blade and upon the socket in Persian and Nastaliq script is gold plated.

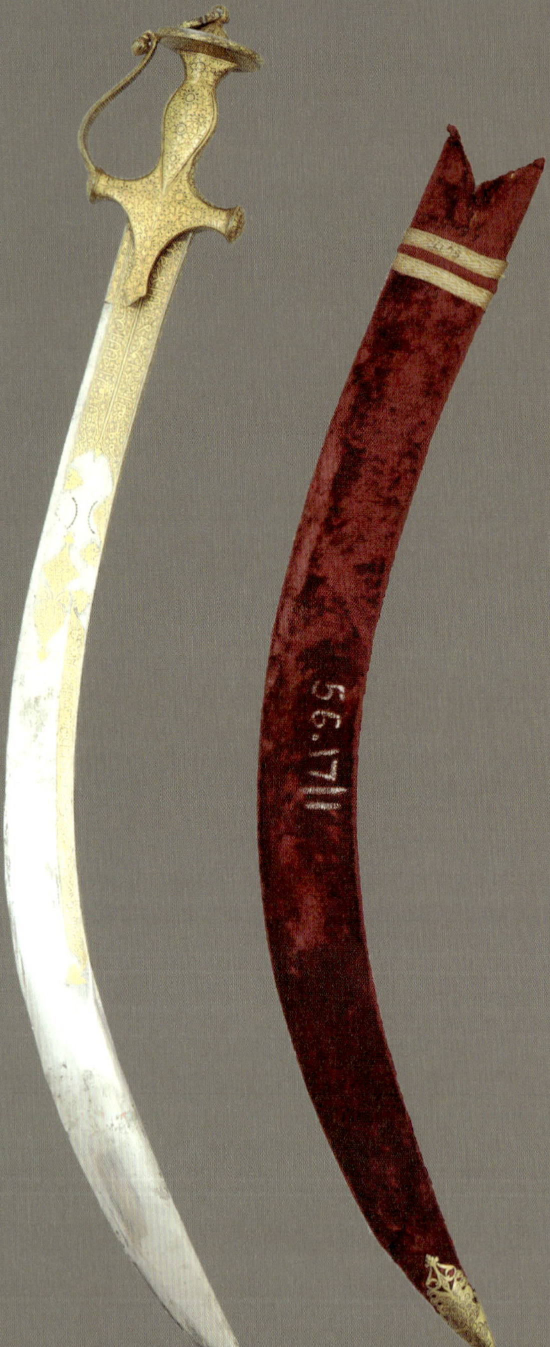
56.1711

Inscribed Sword of Tipu Sultan
c. 1790 CE
Steel
Acc no - 56.17/1

This is the personal sword of Tipu Sultan, the ruler of Mysore; 18th century CE. The Delhishahi hilt with its circular disc pommel, oval grip, small knucle-guard, short quillons and small langets, is damascened in gold with an all-over floral and creeper design. The fine steel blade, devoid of *jauhar*, is inscribed and bears verses from the Holy Quran together with the name of Tipu Sultan and his capital, Srirangapatnam. The wooden sheath is covered with maroon velvet.

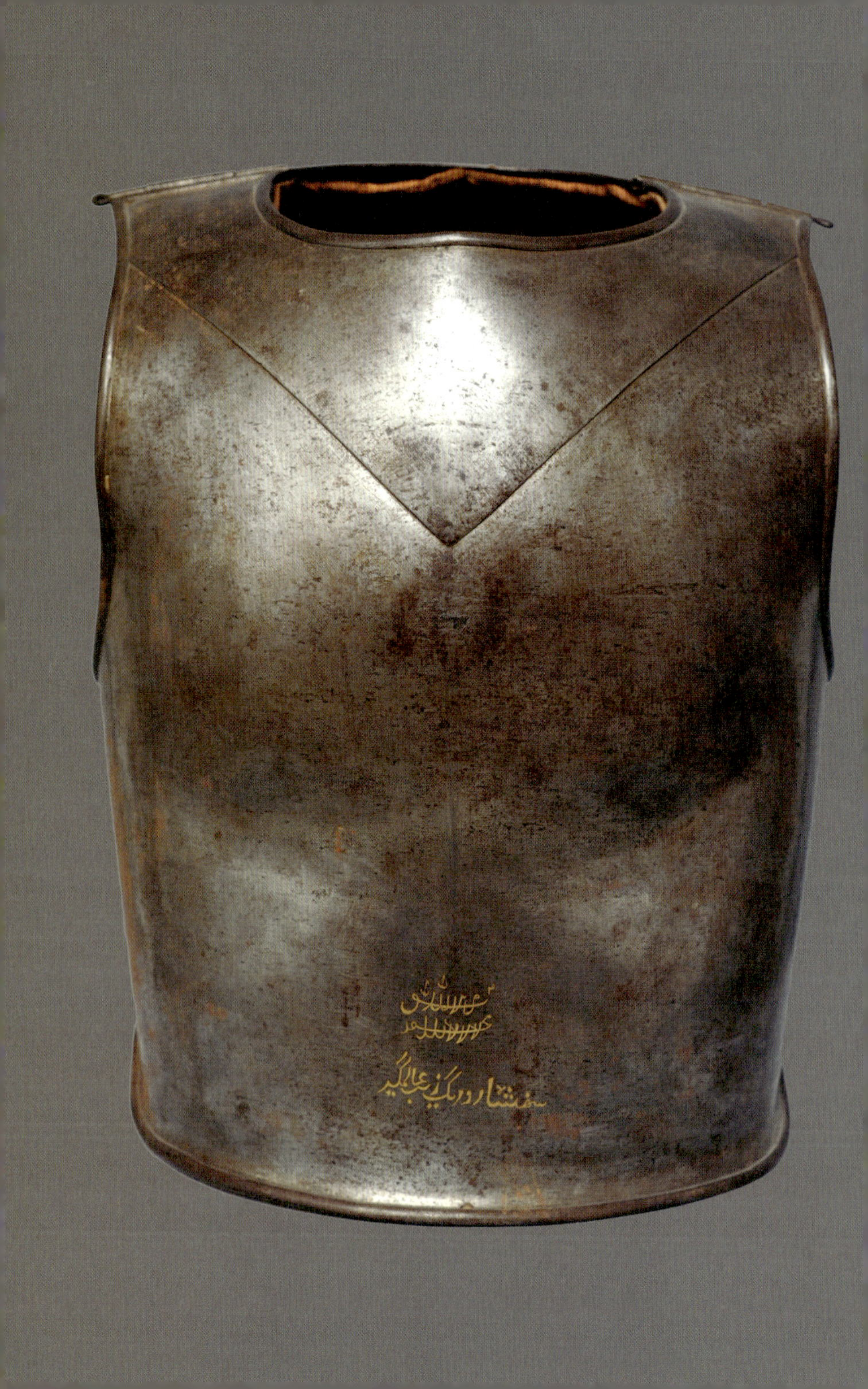

Body Armour of Aurangzeb

c. 1700 CE

Steel

Acc no - 62.2883/2 & 3

This is a waist-coat armour of Aurangzeb (ruled from1658 to 1707 CE.) made of fine Damascus steel. Two plates, one each for the front and the back, are hinged together. Both the plates are detachable.
On lower part of the front plate, a three-lined inscription is engraved in Arabic in Nasakh and Persian in Nastaliq. The name of Aurangzeb is inscribed: Shahanshah Aurangzeb Alamgir. The lining is of yellow quilted satin.

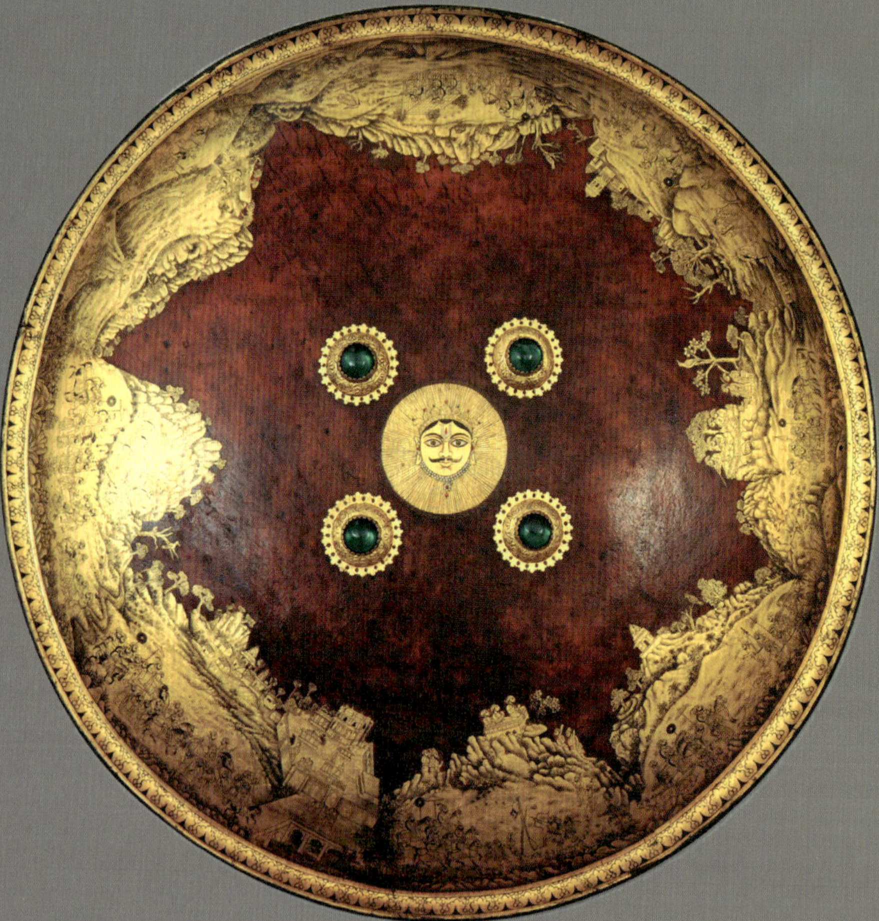

Shield of Maharana Sangram Singh II
c. 1730 CE
Rhino hide
Acc no - 62.2879

This is the personal shield of Maharaja Sangram Singh II of Mewar who ruled from 1710 to 1734 CE. The inscription above the portrait of the prince reads: Marano Sangram Singhji in Devanagari. The shield depicts one of the actual hunting expeditions of the Maharana. The *dhal* is made of rhinoceros hide, lacquered black and painted in brilliant gold, 1730 CE, in the Mewar style of painting.

CENTRAL ASIAN AND PRE-COLUMBIAN ART

The art styles that branched out of Central Asia were influenced by diverse traditions, such as the Hellenistic, Indian, Tibetan, Chinese and Uigurian. Works of art from Central America and Latin America, especially Peru, Mexico and the Honduras, are from the pre-1492 period, when Christopher Columbus, unknowingly, arrived in this part of the world, in search of the new sea route to India and Southeast Asia.

These material remains are testimony to diverse customs, conventions, folklore and beliefs of the people. The Central Asian and pre-Columbian collection comprise artefacts and objects such as wall paintings, painted silk banners, sculpture in wood and stone, stucco and terracotta, coins, porcelain and decorated pottery objects, leather, grass and fibre, precious items of gold and silver, objects used in games, architectural elements, various grave-goods, and religious and secular documents. There are also some beautiful examples of the famous Coptic textiles from Egypt.

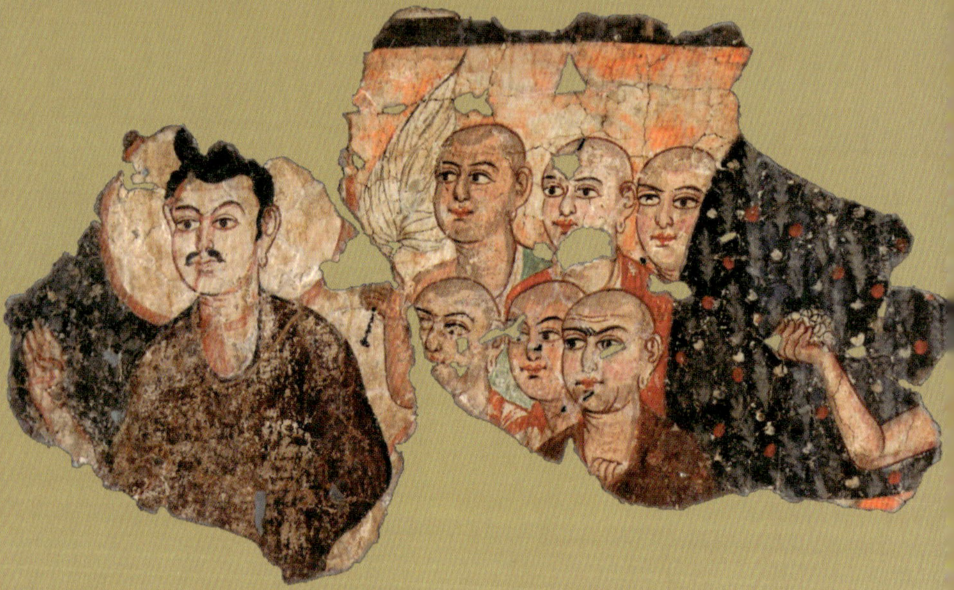

Buddha with Disciples
3rd- 4th century AD
Wall painting
Acc no – M.111.003 (99/1/44)

This is one of the most significant objects in the collection. It is a fragment of a wall painting from a stupa in Miran, in Xinjiang province in China, from 3rd or 4th century CE. The painting preserves only the bust of the Buddha, looking at the spectators, and gesturing with his right hand in *Abhaya Mudra*. He wears a red *sanghati*, an unstitched upper-garment, that covers both shoulders. On his loft arc six monks, his disciples. One of them is holding a *chowrie* or fly whisk. On the left of these monks, is a tree with flowers in full bloom and against it the right arm of a figure can be seen, holding flowers and jewels. Probably, it is a scene from the conversion of six Sakya Princes. The painting shows a strong Hellenistic influence.

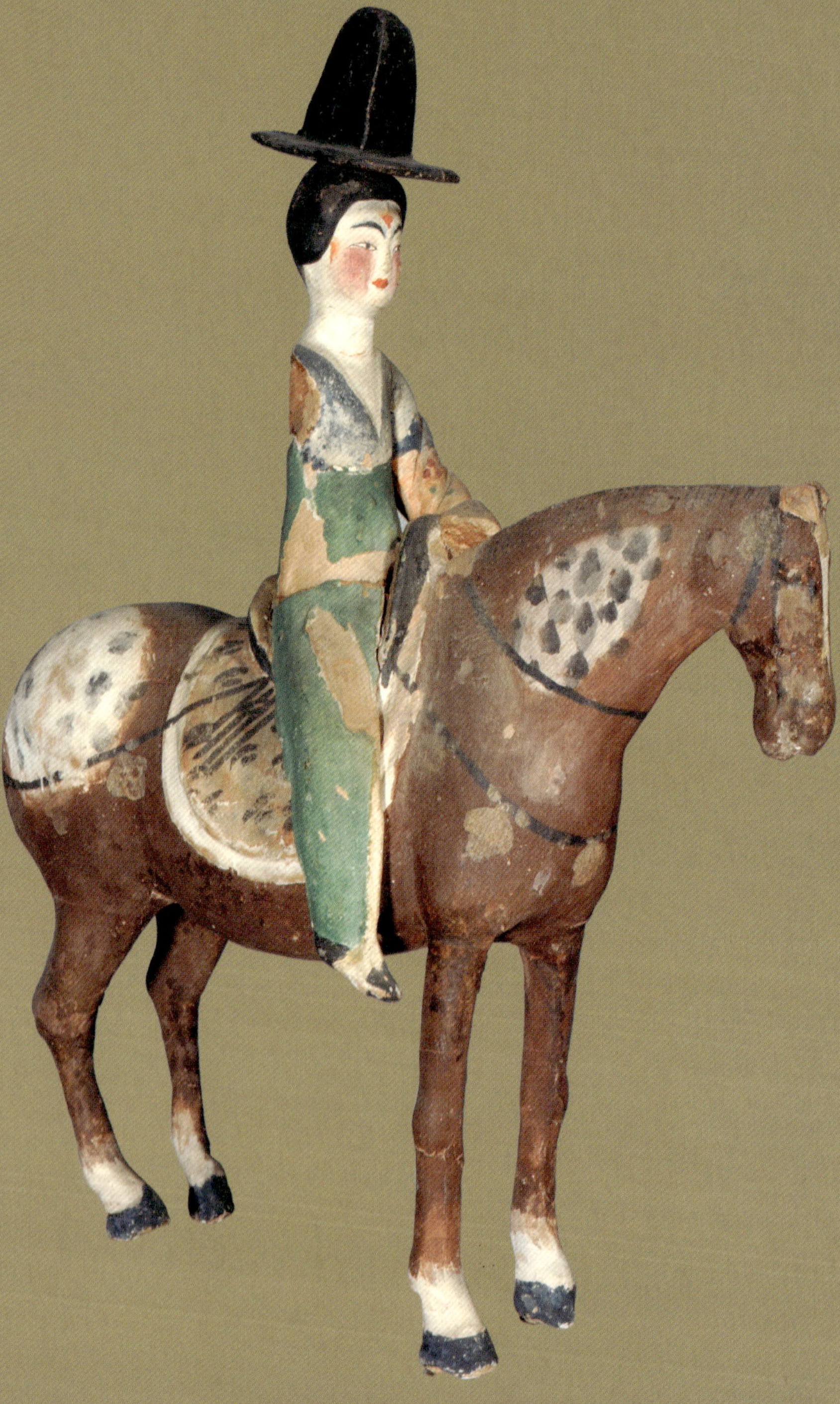

Horse Rider
7th–8th century CE
Stucco
Acc no – Ast.iii.2.016 and Ast.iii.2.022 (2003/7/1922)

This beautiful sculpture depicts a lady horse rider of the T'ang period (618–906 CE). From this particular site of Astana, many horse-riders were found but this was the only example of a lady on a horse. All the mounted figures were evidently meant to symbolise the retinue for the dead in the future abode. The lady and her horse are typically Chinese in style.

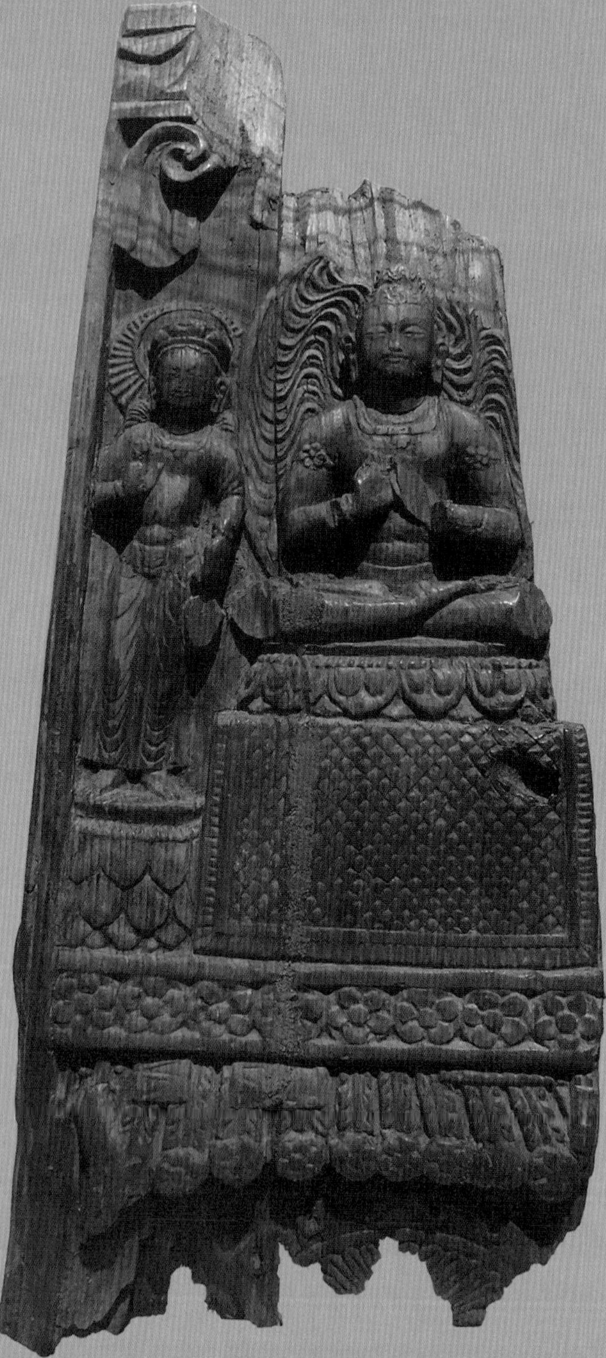

Buddha with Avalokitesvara
6th–7th century CE
Wood
Acc no - Har. 029 (99/6/6)

This is an exquisitely carved wooden panel where the artist has tried to infuse some elements from the silk paintings of Central Asia. The fragment of the wooden panel shows the Buddha seated on a lotus throne in the posture of Vajrasana with his hands in *Vyakhyana Mudra* (explaining posture). On his right, Avalokitesvara is standing on a lotus stand. His right hand is in *Abhaya Mudra*. He is seen holding a vase filed with the eternal *amrit* (*amrtakalasa*). The figures show a Gandharan influence.

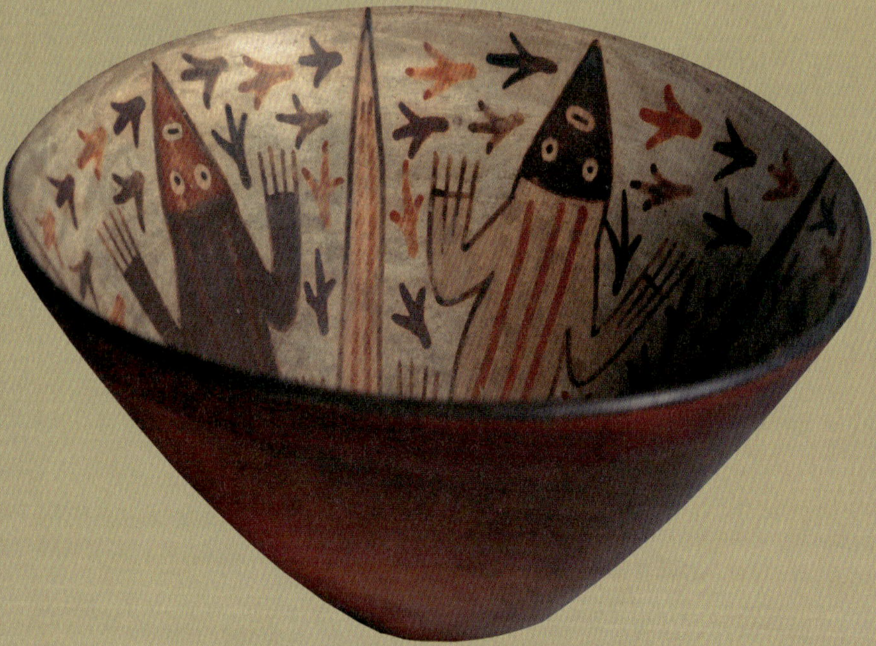

Plate showing Reptiles
300-650 CE
Terracotta
Acc no - 67.335

This shallow bowl painted on the inside has figures of reptiles, repeated in alternate colours of yellow and brown on a white background. Outlines are done by fine brush work in black and dark brown, enhancing the effect of the contour line depending on the colour of the ground. Almost all the vessels from the classic Nazca period are polished smooth so that the slip and design portray the finest glaze.

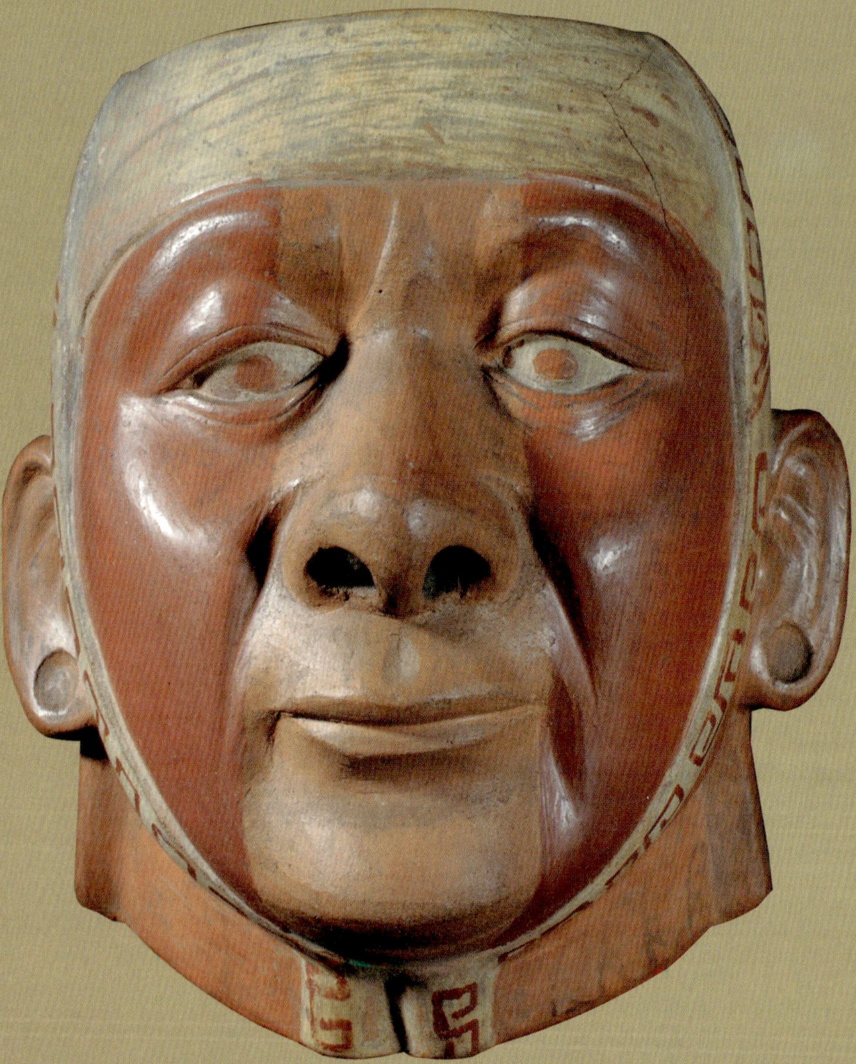

CENTRAL ASIAN AND
PRE COLUMBIAN

Portrait Head Jar
200-700 CE
Clay
Acc no - 67. 246

This head jar is made of natural brown clay with features like the headdress and ornaments incised and painted in reddish brown and buff slips. Vessels in the shape and form of human heads, slightly less than half the natural size, with a wide opening in the top of the head, are so vivid that they look like portraits.

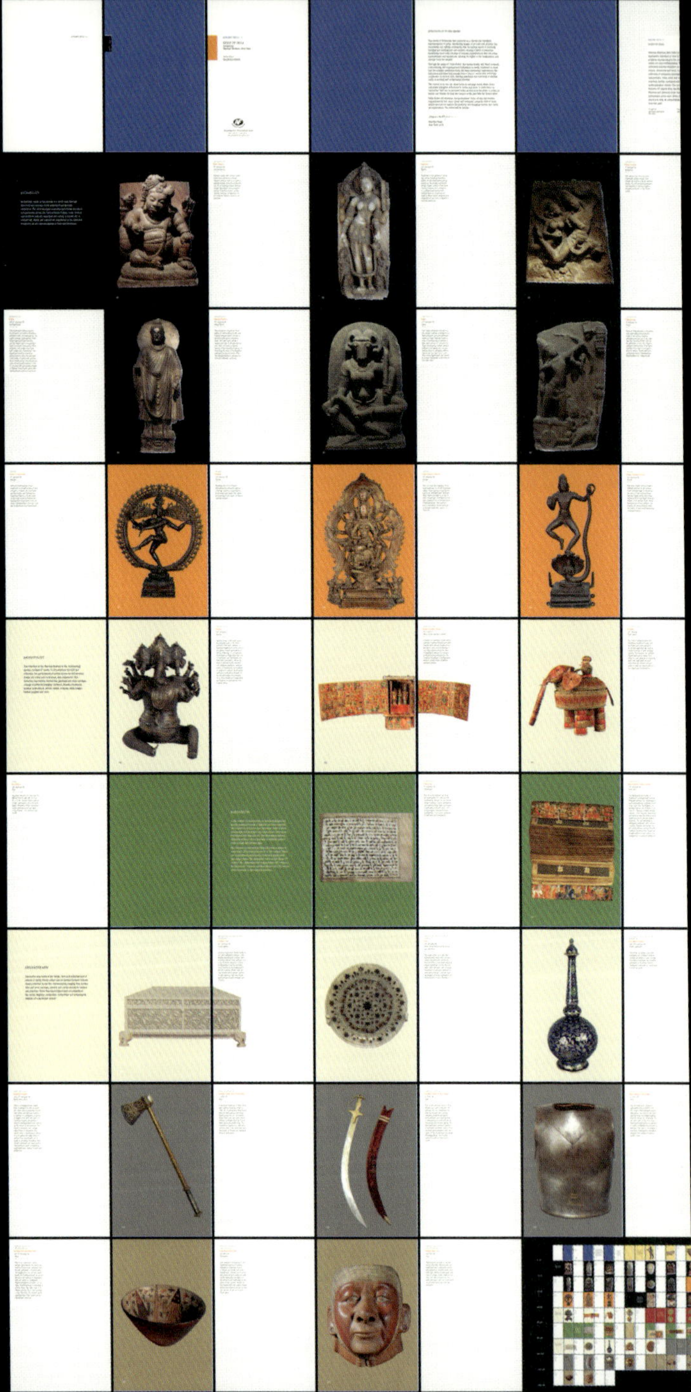

1-16

17-32

33-48

49-64

65-80

81-96

97-112

113-128

129-136

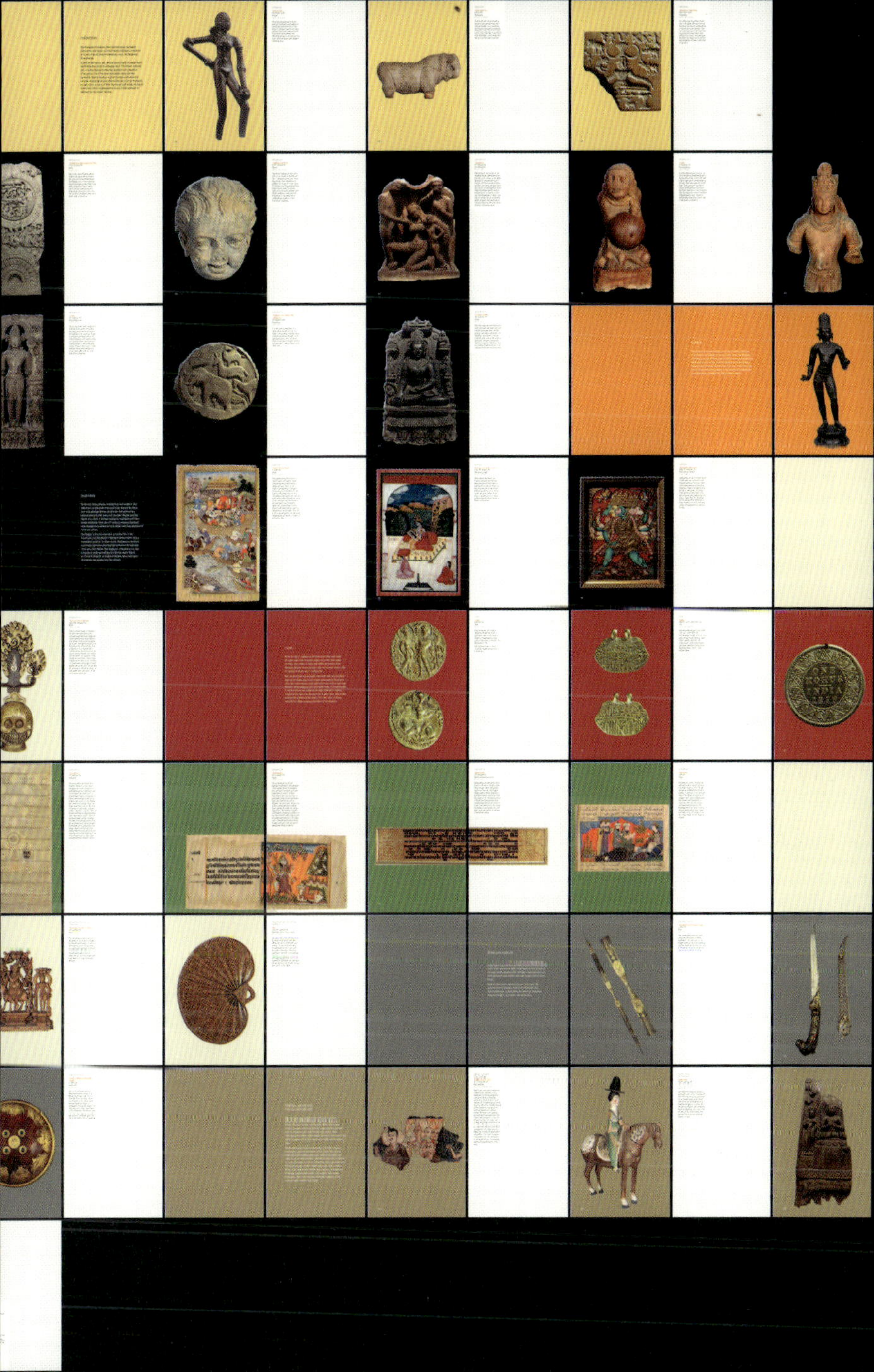

First published in 2015
by
LIMITED EDITIONS
an imprint of

ACADEMIC FOUNDATION

Delhi Sales Office:
4772-73/23 Bharat Ram Road,
(23 Ansari Road), Darya Ganj,
New Delhi - 110 002 (India).
Tel : +91-11-23245001 / 02.
Fax : +91-11-23245005.

Corporate Office:
No. 35, Sector 7,
IMT Manesar,
Gurgaon - 122050.
Haryana (India).
Tel: +91-124-4215070 / 71.

E-mail : books@academicfoundation.com
www.academicfoundation.org

Ageless India, Book 2
Spirit of India
Curated by National Museum, New Delhi

Series Editor: Malvika Singh

ISBN 13: 9789332702028

Designed, printed and bound by
The Book Mint, New Delhi.
www.thebookmint.in